PRAYER
for
People
Who Can't
Sit Still

PRAYER
for
People
Who Can't
Sit Still

William Tenny-Brittian

CHALICE
PRESS

ST. LOUIS, MISSOURI

Biblical quotations, unless otherwise noted, are from the *New Revised Standard Version Bible,* copyright 1989, Division of Christian Education of the National Council of the Churches of Christ in the United States of America. Used by permission. All rights reserved.

Cover art: FotoSearch
Cover and interior design: Elizabeth Wright
Illustration on page 73: FotoSearch

This book is printed on acid-free, recycled paper.

Visit Chalice Press on the World Wide Web at
www.chalicepress.com

10   9   8   7   6   5   4   3   2   1   05   06   07   08   09

Library of Congress Cataloging–in–Publication Data
Tenny-Brittian, William.
   Prayer for people who can't sit still / William Tenny-Brittian.
     p. cm.
   ISBN 13: 978-0-827230-03-6 (pbk. : alk. paper)
   ISBN 10: 0-827230-03-6
   1. Prayer—Christianity. 2. Attention-deficit-disordered adults—Religious life. I. Title.
   BV215.T37 2005
   242'.661968589—dc22
                                                     2004014952
            Printed in the United States of America

Contents

Acknowledgments

I suspect no book is ever written in a vacuum, and this one is certainly no exception (though there were a number of times it was being written *in spite of* a vacuum!). This book would not have been written if Russ White hadn't seen the project and believed in it—I owe my first thanks there.

Next would be my wife, Kris. She stood by me and encouraged me from day one, believing that her ADHD husband really *could* sit still long enough to write a whole book. All that and she spent hours reading and offering suggestions and providing editing tips without complaint. Without her loving support, and the support of all our children, this project would have just been another unrealized good idea. You have blessed me greatly and I love you all.

Then there's my house church family, who allowed me to take the time to tackle this project. You never know how long something's going to take until you're facing a deadline and you have to burn midnight oil. My thanks for their patience.

And finally, I owe a *huge* debt of gratitude to Penelope McCashland, who edited the first drafts of the manuscript. She spent untold hours in a garage office pouring over the rough drafts—and they were pretty rough—and helping me get them to the publisher on time. Many, many thanks.

Introduction

My wife is a contemplative. I watch her pray, and in amazement I have to wonder how she does it. Her eyes close; her face gets a serene, contented look on it, and she sits there. And sits there. And sits there.

She doesn't move.

She doesn't speak.

She just sits there listening and communing with God.

For hours.

Then there's me. I've been a pastor for most of my adult life, and I don't think I've sat still to pray for more than five or ten minutes before something distracts me. I hear a door shut and I'm jolted out of my prayers and start to wonder who came home. The distant sound of an airplane flying sets me to fantasizing about vacationing. And whenever I get distracted, I know my prayer time is over—it's difficult, if not impossible, to reengage.

I thought maybe I wasn't spiritual enough. I felt guilty because I didn't think I was disciplined enough. And so my prayer life was mostly short conversations with God throughout the day—a better compromise than quitting prayer altogether. But through it all, I had this yearning to spend extended times with God. It was something I knew I needed, but I didn't have any idea how to bring it to fruition. So I pretty much gave up.

And then I met Dr. Heather Daniels. Her husband, Terry, had come to help plant a new church and after a few weeks I met his wife. She sized me up in about three minutes and asked me how long I'd been ADHD (Attention Deficit Hyperactivity Disorder).

I blew her off. In my opinion ADHD was a kid's disease treatable by drugs that chemically lobotomized them. I thought most ADHD kids were really just the result of bad parenting anyway. Besides, I surmised, they all eventually grew out of it and went on to become librarians and such. I wasn't ADHD; it wasn't possible.

But her comment stuck in my head—for over a year. During that time she gave my wife an article on dealing with adult spouses with ADHD. She explained to me that many adults indeed have ADHD, that somewhere between 2 and 4 percent of all adults probably suffer from it. And I began to consider the possibility that I might be one of the 4 percent. The more I read and the more I learned about the disorder, the more things began to make sense for me. I remembered my dad telling me that I never sat through a whole church service when I was a child. It wasn't something I remembered, probably because I wasn't traumatized by exasperated parents who tried to make their kid sit still for an hour. Instead, my parents would simply take me out to do something else. Back then, I was just considered a rambunctious little boy who couldn't sit still.

Which was a key to my coming to understand myself. I can't sit still. As I'm writing this I'm aware that my knees are bouncing back and forth like they always do when I'm "sitting still."

But I always thought ADHD kids had trouble in school. I had been a good student. I made great grades all the way through school. How could I be ADHD all these years and be academically successful? Dr. Heather wondered aloud how much more successful I'd be if I'd been diagnosed and treated as a child.

And so I conceded that I was ADHD. It was a difficult concession, but not only did I have all the signs, I realized there were areas in my life that could use a little help.

Like my prayer life. That little itch in my spirit was telling me something, but I didn't have a clue how to scratch it. No one ever thought to tell me there were ways to pray other than sitting still and letting my mind do the talking. I found out by accident.

The Life of Adult ADHD

It's way beyond the scope of this book to talk much about the nuances of adult ADHD, but let me introduce you to a couple of things most people don't know—including most undiagnosed ADHD folks.

Living with ADHD is both a blessing and a curse. I notice almost everything. When I'm driving, I see every sign that I pass. I'm aware of every car on the highway whether it's next to me or half a mile away. And I can probably tell you what the driver's wearing. If it's in my line of sight, I see it. When I stand in front of a store display, I can find what I'm looking for a gazillion times faster than most folks. Oh, and I'm given to exaggeration as well! But it's true that whenever my wife is trying to find her size, style, and color of hosiery on the display stand, it looks to her as if I'd memorized which shelf her brand was on because I reach out and snag exactly what she's looking for almost as an afterthought.

In a restaurant, I'm listening to your conversation. And his. And hers. And theirs. Oh, and I can probably tell you the title and artist of the past two or three songs that were playing on the Muzak in the background. And if I like you, I'll catch the eye of the server and let them know you need a refill on your soda, probably before you realize you need one. I just notice that kind of stuff.

If you know exactly what I'm talking about, you may be ADHD too.

Thom Hartmann in his book *Beyond ADD: Hunting for Reasons in the Past and Present* (Grass Valley, Calif.: Underwood, 1996) has suggested that ADHD is a leftover from ancient humanity. Once upon a time it might have been advantageous for hunters to be highly alert and multisensory aware, in other words to have ADHD. Although he has his dissenters, much of what he has to say makes sense. There are some advantages to having ADHD. Just not too many of them.

My personal assessment of what ADHD is like is that it's a point on a continuum. At the two extremes of the line are "normal" (whatever that is) and "autistic." Someone who suffers from autism is unable to access the filtering mechanisms in the brain. People on the farthest right are aware of virtually every stimulation simultaneously. In my understanding, in the extreme cases, they hear every noise, see every sight, feel every sensation, smell every scent, and even taste the air they breathe with no ability to filter out any of the stimuli. It seems to me that at the other end of the scale is my wife. When she prays she's aware of one thing and one thing only: her connection with God. I think that I could fall down the stairs while carrying a set of kitchen pots and pans, and even with all the clatter she still wouldn't be aware there was anything amiss.

ADHD people are somewhere in between. Our filters can be pretty thin, and this creates a plethora of problems for us. For one, we can be easily distracted. If a conversation is anything but riveting (think algebra, early eighteenth-century poetry, or the story of antique shopping with Wilbur), we may accidentally tune you out when something catches our eye or our ear. It's not that you aren't interesting, but the squirrel that ran across the road and barely missed getting hit by the yellow BMW sports coupe was just screaming for my attention for a moment—sorry, what did you just say?

On the other hand, if we get into a task that calls for high creativity and if we're fascinated in it, we might come to bed at two-thirty in the morning without having stopped for lunch, dinner, or the appointment we had scheduled with you downtown at six—oops.

Another serious problem is that although we see everything, in some ways we see nothing. We miss details others see. For instance, I get in trouble far too often for not only being a bit tactless, but for being insensitive when I've stepped on someone's emotional toes. Everyone else in the room probably saw the grimace of hurt when she asked if the skirt made her look fat and I said it wasn't the skirt. But I didn't, so I expounded on the kind of skirt that would help her look more slender. Then I told her how I tended to wear dark clothes because they easily cover up ten pounds. And as I was about to tell her that by purchasing clothes that were a half-size too big everyone would think she lost weight, my wife kicked me. Hard. That clue I picked up on. The other I didn't. Not because I'm an insensitive jerk, but because I've *never* seen the clues of facial expressions that apparently everyone else sees. But not us ADHD folks.

Living with ADHD is challenging no matter what. I did a year on a medication that gave me the opportunity to learn how to cope better with the issues. I learned better how to pick up on facial and verbal clues. I learned how to tackle tasks more effectively. And I learned to like myself a lot better than I did before, because I finally knew what the deal was.

But no one taught me how to pray.

Kinesthetic Prayer

Kinesthetic prayer is praying using more than just your mouth or your mind. It's using your fingers, hands, feet, and sometimes even your whole body. I learned about kinesthetic prayer quite accidentally. My wife was doing research on a religious movement in Georgia and she invited me to attend with her one afternoon. We drove to a farm south of Atlanta where, according to the press, twenty-five thousand of us gathered to hear a woman bring us a message from the Virgin

Mary. We weren't Roman Catholic, but someone gave each of us a rosary, and we sat in the middle of a field with the other pilgrims praying the "Our Father" prayer over and over.

After an hour or so, I realized I was staying in touch with the praying. Using the beads on the rosary in counting the prayers had a satisfying tactile sense to it. The beads moving through my fingers provided just enough sensory stimulation to keep me focused on praying. It was a revelation that was pretty well lost on me at the time, though. Probably the fact that prayer beads weren't typically associated with non-Catholics got in the way of my discovery, and I did not revive the practice in my own life for many years.

My breakthrough moment came when I walked a labyrinth about a year after I'd been diagnosed. The ancient practice of labyrinth walking had experienced a revival during the late '90s and I did some research into the phenomenon. In 2001 I actually constructed the first labyrinth I ever walked, because there weren't any available locally. I spent forty minutes of some of the best prayer time I'd ever experienced as I slowly made my way to the labyrinth's center and back. For the first time in my prayer-life I literally could feel the presence of God for an extended period of time. God was *so* there. It was amazing.

Suddenly it all came to me. I remembered the prayer beads. I thought about the times I felt close to God when I was writing. And I understood why God seemed to show up when I was busy doing something while I prayed. I was a kinesthetic pray-er.

Prayer for Those Who Can't Sit Still

This book was written for those who feel the need to get connected with God in prayer, but can't sit still long enough to do it. I'm convinced that prayer is one of the most powerful tools in our arsenal, but one of the most underutilized. Prayer changes things. For one, it changes my heart and enlivens my spirit. For another, whenever I've been in the presence of God, I come away with a sense of well-being that is nearly indescribable. And I've seen enough prayers answered that I'm one of the crowd who believes our prayers somehow empower a Godly response.

But I'm also one of the crowd who believes that if our prayers are going to be effective, we are going to have to spend some time with the Divine Presence. I suspect that most of us would have a lousy relationship with our spouses, our kids, our friends, or our wider families if we only spent the amount of time with them that we spend with God. How can we build a serious relationship with anyone, let alone God, if we spend less than three minutes a day with the person? A relationship takes time together.

That time together doesn't have to be sit-still time. Some of the best hours spent with my wife are when we walk together. Why wouldn't that be true of time with God?

So this book offers ten different kinesthetic prayers for those who want to get into God's presence, but don't have the contemplation gene.

In doing research for this book, however, I discovered a side benefit. Many of these kinesthetic prayers work well with children—ADHD or not. In my experience, kids don't sit still any better than I do, so when I took the ideas for kinesthetic prayer to Junior Camp, with children ages nine through twelve, I was surprised at how much they got out of praying when we exposed them to these tools. In some cases we saw serious heart-felt prayers offered with tears and weeping as these children connected with God on perhaps the deepest level they'd ever experienced. It was a moving experience both for child and camp counselor.

So whether you use this book for your personal prayer life, or to introduce kinesthetic prayer to your children, children's ministry, or youth group, my prayer for you is that the experience brings you closer to God than ever before.

CHAPTER I

The Joy of Journaling

I've been journaling my prayers on and off since 1997.
Currently, I'm in one of my "on" times and wonder why I ever
put the pen down. Although I don't put pen to paper every day,
I'm consistent enough at it that I'm really happy with what I do.

But it hasn't always been that way. My wife bought me my
first journal for Christmas in 1997. She also gave me a devotional
book to go along with it, so for my 1998 New Year's resolution,
I decided to keep a daily journal. It was a short-lived resolution.
I quickly ran out of steam, or discipline, as the case may be. I
made only three consecutive daily entries before I started missing
a day here, a day there. I set my pen down and quit by January
21. The last line of my 1998 journaling experience reads: "I
hope/pray I'll find a better prayer life than I currently have."

Failure is in the eye of the beholder, I always say. Although
I wanted a better prayer and journaling life, I never looked at
what I'd done as a failure, just a false start. In 1999 I started
journaling again, only this time I resolved that if I quit, that
would be okay. So I started writing. And then I stopped. But

because I hadn't beaten myself up for it, a couple of months later I started again. By 2000 I'd become consistent enough in my journaling that I could go back and read with great joy the things that had touched me during the previous year. I was a journaler!

Journaling isn't new. Cave walls around the world have paintings and etchings recording ancient everyday life events. Much later, in the fourth century, Augustine of Hippo wrote the book *Confessions,* widely considered the first autobiography, and a forerunner of the modern-day journal. Later, in tenth-century Japan, women began keeping pillow-books that chronicled these women's hopes, their dreams, snippets of gossip, and daily events. Beginning in the Victorian age of England, both men and women began recording their thoughts and reflections in journals that resemble our modern-day journals and diaries. These journals recorded some of the most innocuous and mundane details about their lives, but also contained deep and powerful reflections on their thoughts. It is this kind of reflection that provides a gateway to journaling as kinesthetic prayer.

Journaling as Kinesthetic Prayer

People who can't sit still need to be doing something in order to accomplish something else. In my case, it's like my body and my mind cannot work independently; instead they have to be doing something together. So when the pastor says, "Let's bow our heads and pray" my mind gets ready to tune out, anticipating the moments of stillness during the prayer. For many of us, when it comes to praying, movement is as important as the words we offer.

Journaling is one way I can stay tuned in to prayer. Although some prefer using a computer for their journaling, I particularly enjoy using pen and paper. I like the feel and the look of ink marrying itself to a page. In either case, the act of kinesthetically creating words to express yourself can move you into a place of quiet reflection and even contemplation.

On the other hand, some may need more stimulation than just a pen and tablet. Younger children and some of us with a high level of hyperactivity may find journaling to be just a bit too sedate. If you think this describes you, there are plenty of more active prayers in later chapters; however, I would invite you to try journaling for a week to see if it works for you. I was surprised. Once I learned how to effectively use my journal as a prayer tool, I discovered just how meaningful my writing can be and how close I found myself to God.

The ABCs of Journaling as Prayer

Journaling is a rather simple task that may need little introduction for some. On the other hand, journaling as a prayer exercise has a slightly different nuance than writing in your diary so that you can remind yourself of what you did today when you read about it four years from now.

There are only two parts to journaling as prayer: the tools you use and the text you write.

The Tools of Journaling

Whenever you journal, consider that you're participating in the world of creativity. Writing is an art form, and there can be something intrinsically satisfying about crafting words that reflect deep and sometimes profound meaning. When it comes to journaling as prayer, you will want to be doubly aware that what you are doing has significance. The words you write are addressed from your heart to the Divine Spirit, and though God is pleased whenever you're in conversation, you will want to put your best foot forward. So no matter what form of prayer journaling you use, consider choosing tools of quality, if for no other reason than to remind yourself of the importance of what you're doing.

Depending on what works best for you, there are two basic sets of tools for prayer journaling: pen and paper, or a computer. We'll deal with the tool sets separately, since there are advantages and disadvantages to both.

A few of the author's journals

I have tried pen and paper, as well as using a computer, for journaling. For me, there's nothing like gripping a pen and pouring out my thoughts on paper. Although there are any number of tablets, diaries, and journals available at any office supply, stationary, or book store, once you get started journaling, you may find yourself gifted with an almost endless supply of journals from friends and relatives. Personally, I prefer journals that lay flat when I write on them, rather than those that bow from the middle as many bound journaling books do.

Most journals are not prohibitively expensive—you can pick one up in almost any bookstore or office supply store. However, there are some really nice alternatives for those with more discretionary income. Handmade journals have gained popularity over the past few years. These journals not only have artistic covers, but many are bound with handmade paper that has a unique texture. These handmade journals are often available at local art shows and online. However, no matter what kind of journal you use, whether store-bought or handmade, I recommend getting one with acid-free paper so that you leave a legacy that will last.

When it comes to writing instruments, the sky's the limit and the choices are almost endless. Today you can buy pens and pencils not only in a variety of colors, but with a variety of scents, textures, and even metallic glitter. These are not only pleasing to use, but are pleasing to the eye. Fountain pens are also a luxury item that can make your writing literally flow. However, on a personal note, I've tried to use fountain pens only to discover that I make more of a mess than not. Regardless of what you use, some care in the writing, as well as the medium, can elevate your writing to something beyond simply your thoughts, but truly a work of art on multiple levels.

Then there is computer journaling. The use of computers in journaling has become relatively common over the past few years. A majority of people in the U.S. have access to a computer, and computer literacy is rising rapidly. Journaling on a computer is every bit as kinesthetic as using pen and ink. There is something instinctively satisfying when fingers fly across the keyboard and words appear on the screen.

There are dozens of word processing programs that are useful journaling tools. Many programs have a password protect feature that allows you to maintain your privacy. There are also special journaling software programs such as *Life Journal* and VistaWrite's *Journal*. You can find both of these at latebloomerpublishing.com. Cosmi makes a journaling program called *Portable Journal* that works on both computer and PDA platforms for those of us married to mobility. The advantage of software journaling programs is that they can be helpful in stimulating the writing process. However, the disadvantage is that they may force your writings into artificial directions rather than pointing your mind toward prayer.

Recently, the phenomenon of "blogging" has come to the forefront of computer journaling. The word *blog* is a contraction of the term "Web Log." A blog is a journal that is generally posted online for the world to see. I used a blog for a while, but in the end decided I wasn't quite as open, honest, and transparent using it as I was when I knew God and I were the only ones who were likely to read my entries. On the other hand, blogging can be quite cathartic, since the whole world is invited to share in your joys, anxieties, hopes, and fears. There are a number of blogging Web sites available online, but you can find the most used site at www.blogger.com.

The Art of Journaling

Different prayer journaling styles fit a variety of needs. Some of these will catch your fancy, and others may not. I would invite you to try each one a couple of times. You will find that you use one or two styles regularly, but the others are helpful when you are looking for specific results.

Devotional Prayer Journaling

For those of us who can't sit still, the thought of "having" to do devotions can be agonizing. For most of us, "doing devotions" means we have to find a quiet place with few distractions so that we can read a sacred text—whether that be the Bible or some other writing that moves our soul—then read some sort of devotional book to help our first reading "assignment" make sense, and finally we have to try to sit still and pray silently for some unspecified, but lengthy, period of time. Some have even tried to add journaling to the to-do list of daily devotionals.

Devotional prayer journaling, however, can actually be a kinesthete's joy. I like to do my devotional prayer journaling in my local coffee shop, where the distractions are plentiful. Armed with a copy of a sacred text, my journal, and a pen, I take over a table with a muffin and latte in hand. This takes a lot of the regimen out of my devotions and I find I can relax and spend quality time with the Divine.

To practice devotional prayer journaling, begin with a quiet prayer asking God to speak to you through your reading and writing. Then take a few minutes to find your center by closing your eyes, breathing deeply, and listening to your heart. I tend to take a sip of my sugar-free, hazelnut, fat-free, single ristretto, no-foam latte and then close my eyes as I savor the flavor. In those moments, I take a few deep breaths and focus my thoughts on God. When I open my eyes, I am ready to read reflectively, as you will be too. As you do, "listen" to your spirit to see which words or passages catch your interest or imagination. Underline or highlight these lines. You may even want to jot a few notes in the margins to remind you of whatever caught your eye.

When you finish reading (and in a coffee shop that could take awhile), go back and reflect on what you've underlined. Then you are ready to begin your journaling exercise. One of the most effective tools I've discovered is a simple three-part journaling exercise I call R^3 ("R Cubed") that can help you focus on what God may be saying to you through the sacred writings.

The three Rs are *Recall, Reflect,* and *Respond.* (See page 17 for an example of an R^3 journal entry.)

RECALL

As you look back over those passages that jumped out at you, choose the one that seems to be making the most urgent claim on your spirit. Copy this passage and its reference in your journal. You will want to do this so that when you reread your writings in the future, you won't have to try to ferret out whatever sacred writing you used in order for the journal entry to make sense.

REFLECT

When you've finished copying the passage, let your pen take over as you begin to reflect on why this passage was calling your name. What caught your attention? Was it disturbing? confusing? Did it evoke an emotional response? Is something going on in your life that this passage may relate to? As you reflect on the passage, begin to steer your writing toward what this passage is saying to you. What is God trying to teach you? How does this passage relate to your life? What are you feeling called to do? How will you respond? This last question is the one that leads to the final part of the journaling exercise.

Respond

Begin to wind down your writing by offering a written prayer—a commitment—to the Divine. This can be as brief as a single sentence, while at other times you may let it go on for a page or more, depending on how you were touched during your writing. The goal of this section is to respond honestly to what you've felt and heard during your reading and writing. If you're feeling contrite, let your writing reflect that. If you're angry, let God know. I've learned that whenever my response is not absolutely honest, my writing rings hollow and my journal entry leaves me unsatisfied, as if my prayer time was empty. However, if you're willing to be completely honest, even if your honesty seems not-so-nice, God will honor your time and you will find that you go away thoughtful and fulfilled. Don't forget, you can always go back later to write more as you process your feelings.

Event Journaling

A second journaling exercise to try is event journaling. It's been said that life is 10 percent what happens to you, and 90 percent how you respond to the 10 percent. Many of us don't take the time to reflect on what's happening in our lives, so we regularly miss the opportunity to benefit from life's lessons.

To experience this form of prayer, use the R^3 format described above to get started. Although you can journal about any event in your life, I've discovered the ones that make the most impact are those where I've made a mess of things. For those of us who can't sit still, this often means doing or saying something that was less than appropriate, often without even knowing it. When we find out what we've done, event journaling is one of the best tools to reflect and learn from the incident.

R³ Journaling

Recall

What scripture touched or intrigued you? Write it here.

(Gal. 4:6–7) Because you are sons, God sent the Spirit of his Son into our hearts, the Spirit who calls out, "Abba, Father." So you are no longer a slave, but a son; and since you are a son, God has made you also an heir.

Reflect

What is it that touched or intrigued you? Reflect on that here.

Abba is Greek for daddy, like what a little kid calls their father. When I read this passage I had to wonder what it would be like to have a relationship with God like that. I tend to see God as so much bigger and royal and awesome to think that God can be like a daddy. But it isn't me who calls God daddy, but the Spirit. It may be beyond me to be able to fathom God's "daddy-ship," but the Holy Spirit gets it, and as Paul wrote in Romans 8:26, when we don't know how to pray, the Spirit takes over on our behalf. I think I'd like to have God as a daddy. He's already my Lord, Savior, and God, but I want that intimate relationship Paul speaks of here where I'm not just a son, but a child in God's arms.

Respond

Write your prayer response to these insights here.

God, the notion of being your child young, innocent, and just childlike is beyond my "gone-to-college and more" intellect. Help me to let go of my intellect enough to allow you to be my Abba—my daddy. Amen

Begin by finding your center and then prayerfully recalling the event. Record the event in as much detail as you can remember. It's easy to retell the event without being totally honest, so make it a habit to be painfully truthful about your words and actions. When you've finished this, pause for a few moments to ask the Divine to help you learn from your experience, and then begin writing your reflection.

As you reflect, ask yourself a couple of questions. What was your part in the event? What did you do right and what could you have handled better? Reflect on how you'd have preferred the event to unfold and find its resolution. Then take some time to ponder what you could have done to bring about that preferred resolution. Be open to the still, small voice or nudging of God as you write. Your reflections should include your innermost thoughts and insights as you wrestle with God about the situation.

As you begin to wind up your reflections, try to synthesize what you've discovered into a single sentence. This should be your "Aha!" of what you've learned from reflecting on the event. Over the years you may find yourself repeating these same "aha!" lessons, to your own chagrin. When I've looked back over my own journal and realized I've written the same "aha's!" over and over again, I discover I am more firmly resolved to not repeat the same mistake another time. Miraculously, it seems, when I write these reflections in my journal I find that I begin to make the same mistake a little less frequently.

Finally, take the time to respond. What is it you need to do to follow-up with this event? Do you need to make amends, make a personal change in your habits, or make a connection with someone you've avoided? Write these thoughts in the form of a prayer, committing your actions, words, and what you've learned before God.

Other R³ Journaling Exercises

There are a number of other R³ journaling exercises that you can put to good use. All of these use the R³ format of *Recall,*

Reflect, and *Respond* in order to help focus your heart and mind on prayer.

Dream journaling has long been a part of the journaling genre. I keep a separate dream journal next to the bed, with a lighted pen by it, to jot down any midnight dreams that awaken me. You will discover that by jotting down the details in a bedside dream journal and then applying the R^3 journaling tools the next day in your regular journal, you will be better able to process your dreams. Sometimes you may discover meanings or deep-seated concerns in your dreams, while at other times you may hear God speaking about some task before you. In any event, the practice of R^3 journaling can help you to understand your deepest thoughts and emotions and help commit them to God.

Another journaling technique I practice comes from my reading habits. Many of us read a near overdose prescription of self-help books on leadership, spirituality, and the like. At the end of many of the chapters in these books are study guides with questions that most of us seldom take the time to reflect on while reading the book. I invite you to jot the questions down on sticky-notes and stick them on the inside cover of your journal for later. Make a habit of glancing over the questions (for example, Who is the most effective leader whom you followed?) regularly to see if one of them catches your spirit. When it does, prayerfully apply the R^3 pattern to the question as you journal.

Over the years, this has given me an incredible wealth of insights into my own spiritual and emotional life. This exercise can help all of us become better persons as we reflect on who we are in relationship to our world and with God.

Journaling Letters to God

Another style of journaling is writing a letter to God. For many people, prayer is more like a letter than a conversation, so journaling a letter to God can be a natural extension of that experience.

Journaling a letter to God is not unlike writing a letter to a friend, except that it doesn't take a stamp or an e-mail address. To journal a letter to God, begin as if you were writing any other letter: "Dear God." Most of the time when we write a letter, we spend an inordinate amount of space on small talk. However, if you're going to write a letter to the Divine, consider getting right to the point. Whether you're going to ask God for a favor, a blessing, or some other request, don't spend a lot of time mincing words.

As you write, consider spending some extra time trying to convince God of whatever it is you're asking for. This isn't so much to convince God to relent, but to clarify that you really understand what you're praying. Sometimes as you write these letters, you may begin to understand that you really don't need or want what you're asking for. On the other hand, there are times when you will discover just how badly you depend on God and you may be moved to break into a paragraph of gratitude. Whatever the emotions you feel as you write, get them down on paper. The Divine already knows your heart; you're just illuminating your feelings.

Again, as you're writing, try to keep attuned to your spirit in order to hear God speaking as you write and reflect. That way, if you sense God giving you an answer, you can adjust the letter writing to suit your heart.

Journaling a Conversation with God

Of all the journaling styles I engage in, this is the one that takes the most time, fills up the most pages in my journal, and often yields the best results. Journaling a conversation means to literally write down the words you would be saying aloud if you and God were having a one-on-one conversation.

Typically, I journal conversations with God in the midst of when I'm using some other style. In the middle of a paragraph I'll realize that I'm engaged in a two-way conversation. It generally begins when I've written a line or two as a prayer and I hear that still, small inner voice within me responding. So I'll write what I've heard and then respond to that. As I do, I realize that I'm writing a full conversation with God.

These conversations often happen when I'm in a place to "discuss my life" with God, meaning that I have something I need to talk over with God. It may be about a decision I need to make, it may be a personal issue I'm dealing with, or it may be a mood I'm in. But invariably they just begin.

Below is an example of a conversation I recently journaled. Notice that the conversation began in the midst of a reflection.

> I get caught up in the nonessentials—except that everything I'm doing right now is essential. So here I am. Haven't cracked my Bible yet…waiting for God to lead. But God asks if I'm going to follow if He leads? I say, "Yes." He says, "then why are you worrying and fretting?"
>
> "Because if I can't trust *me* to do what needs to get done, how can I trust you?"
>
> "So, you've created me in *your* image?"
>
> "I guess so," I respond. And I think, *how absurd.* Then I wonder, *just how real is the Lord? a figment?* No, I've seen the Lord work and I've felt His presence.
>
> "Clearly that's more than you could manage on your own."
>
> "Yes, but you're asking me to walk blindly," I add limply.
>
> "Who's driving?"
>
> "I am."
>
> "How's that working for you?"

The conversation goes on for three handwritten pages, but in the end I respond by making a commitment to surrender the steering wheel of my life, at least regarding the issue I was dealing with at the time.

To engage in this kind of exercise, you have to be willing to allow the voice in your mind to speak through your writing. Begin by finding a good centering place and then turn your attention to God. This is critical in this exercise, since you'll want to be fully attuned to the voice of the Divine rather than to your own thoughts. When you feel fully secure in God's presence, begin by writing a prayer thought. Then pause and listen to your heart to see if there is some response. If there is, write this down in the words you hear. Then respond to this thought, and so on.

Probably the most important thing to do happens when you've finished the conversation. When you are done, go back and read what you've written. Reflect on the words and whether they are from God or from your own center of the universe. This can be tricky, but a good rule of thumb is that God is the author and sustainer of love and anything not of love is not of God.

Conversational journaling isn't for everyone, but it can be both exciting and rewarding. The key is to listen to the three voices in your head and be sure you can identify which one is yours, which one is God's, and which one is evil, Satan, the dark side, or whatever you call those forces that would deceive your spirit and soul. When you pay attention to the source of your thoughts. It can make all the difference in the world.

Two Words of Caution

There are a couple of cautions about journaling we all need to be aware of. The first is a legal issue. Journals have been subpoenaed in a number of court cases in the past, so be aware that what you write could end up in the public eye if you should end up being accused of some heinous crime (not likely, I hope, if you're journaling prayer on a consistent basis).

The second caution has to do with your inevitable end. We are all going to die, and that's something we all have to face up to. If you journal regularly, and if you're not using a computer with password protection, then one day your journal entries may fall into the hands of your spouse, your children, or your grandchildren unless you've taken steps to insure otherwise.

If your journal entries need to go to the grave with you, it will be helpful to let a trusted friend or family member know that well in advance of your demise. There are a number of ways to let folks know about your final wishes, including a will. But unless you tell someone what to do with your journals, they may well find their way into some grieving family member's hands.

As for myself, I know that some of what I've written is both personal and a bit embarrassing, but I realize that my words might bring a measure of hope to some family member one day. I've learned that whatever may befall me, I can trust in God to help me along, and this gets written into my journal regularly. So through all the ups and downs of my journal, anyone who reads it will know that I was fallible; but they will also know that I trusted the God to whom I devoted not only my life, but also many pages of my writing.

CHAPTER 2

I Hope You Dance

Almost everyone dances in church. Whenever music gets going that touches the heart, whether it's the thumping of a bass guitar or the chords of the pipe organ, people in the congregation begin to dance. It can be very subtle, like feet tapping or bodies swaying, but the body begins to dance in spite of us.

Dancing as an expression of worship predates churches by thousands of years. There are petroglyphs nearly five thousand years old that portray dancers at worship. There are plenty of biblical dancers recorded as well, including Miriam, Jephthah's daughter, and King David, plus there are a number of exhortations to dance found in the Psalms.

Apparently, dancing regularly took place in the church even during the first few centuries. According to both Justin Martyr in the second century and Hippolytus in the third century, circle dances were a part of the church's liturgy. By the fourth century, however, church leaders believed that the practice of religion should be an intellectual decision, not an aesthetic delight, so dance fell into disfavor.

In the twentieth century dance in worship regained popularity. In the early 1900s, for example, Ted Shawn and Ruth St. Denis choreographed dances specifically suitable for church. Dance has slowly become more accepted in some churches, but usually as a performance art rather than as a participatory act. In most worship services, if there is a dancer gracefully moving across the stage, the audience watches in hushed awe, almost as if they were at a ballet. It is both a beautiful and awe-inspiring event, and no doubt the dancer experiences a keen sense of the Divine in the performance. However, both the dancer and the congregation would likely be in shock if someone like me, all six feet tall and two hundred and too many pounds, got up to join in. Dance as kinesthetic prayer is performed unto God.

Dance as Kinesthetic Prayer

Movement and touch are the twin foundations for the kinesthete, and dance is a movement-rich activity. Typically, you need only a beat and a joyful heart to engage in dance as prayer; however, there are times and circumstances when you need neither. Dance is simply the physical manifestation of what the heart, mind, and/or spirit is striving to communicate.

You will need to consider a number of aspects when making your decision to practice dance as prayer. The first is whether you're planning on practicing this form of prayer in public worship. If you are, you will need to decide how demonstrative you want to be in your prayer. A number of churches today welcome dance as prayer; on the other hand, as of this writing, the majority of churches may react a bit less favorably. In the latter cases, you will want to speak with the pastor and the worship leaders before you spontaneously break into dance steps during the weekly worship service. On the other hand, if your dance prayer is relatively subdued, there shouldn't be much of an issue, unless you plan on standing in the front row so everyone can see you.

The second consideration is whether or not you will be using any dance accessories, such as ribbons, streamers, flags, or tambourines. These liturgical dance accessories are readily available at a number of outlets, and flags and ribbons can also be easily produced at home. However, ribbons, streamers, and flags demand significant space for waving and twirling, and tambourines require a situation where making some extra noise isn't going to be an issue.

Another consideration is the question of music. For most occasions, dance is a music-dependent art form. Without a beat or a rhythm, it is difficult for most of us to get our bodies into motion. However, those with keen senses can often pick up on natural rhythms, and those with ADHD may well be able to express these rhythms easier than others, simply because they cannot tune them out. For these folks, music may not be necessary to initiate a prayer dance.

However, for the majority of us, music is probably a necessity for practicing dance as prayer. At home, choose the music that moves your heart. Every generation has its own beat, one that sounds "real" to them. The music that moves my dad's feet hardly gets me up from my seat. On the other hand, the music that touches my spirit irritates my dad and drives my own teenagers from the room. However, I take great comfort in knowing that my grandchildren will one day cover their ears when my son turns up the radio in his house!

Regardless of what genre of music moves your heart, there is a spiritual cognate just waiting for you at your music store. From the great hymns of the past to rock-n-roll, R&B, and rap, there is edifying music being produced that can move your spirit into an attitude of prayer. And don't eschew whatever contemporary, secular music dares to touch you. I remember clearly dancing to Cat Stevens's "I Want to Live in a Wigwam" and offering it as a thank-you prayer as he sang, "I'm glad I'm alive, am I" and crying out with a petition for ongoing guidance with "Gotta get to heaven, get a guide." Today, a number of great songs coming over the airwaves carry a heavy dose of spirituality within them, even those that aren't necessarily meant to be spiritual. When a song strikes your soul and you can offer the words as a prayer, consider adopting it into your repertoire.

Learning to Dance Spontaneously

I've never been a great dancer. In high school I wasn't the one the gals fought over to get the next dance. On the other hand, I can hardly keep my feet still when the music begins to play. Prayer dancing does not necessitate taking lessons in order to practice the prayer effectively.

Choreographing for a performance is different than offering a spontaneous prayer in dance. It can be a rather simple thing to just let your feet, arms, hands, and head carry you away in movement to the rhythms around you, whether from the natural rhythms or from the music. The movements don't necessarily need to have any specific meanings attached to them, so long as they are expressions of what your heart and spirit are trying to convey to God.

If you've never danced spontaneously, this may seem completely foreign, but if you can appreciate a beat—even if you can't keep a beat—you can learn to dance your prayers. It's probably easiest to begin in the privacy of your own home, whether in a back room or the living room. Move the furniture so you have a clear space in the middle of the room and then put a song on the stereo that you know gladdens your heart and maybe even bubbles a prayer to your consciousness. Stand in the middle of the room and close your eyes. Listen to the music and pay attention to your natural physical response. You may find your head bobbing, your feet or toes tapping, or even your whole body swaying. As you become aware of these physical responses, begin to accentuate them as you add other parts of your body to the rhythms.

Although there are no rules for spontaneous prayer dancing, there are some natural gestures that are universal. Raising hands above your head embodies reaching out for God as well as a gesture of surrender. Cupping your hands before you, or stretching out your hands palms up, symbolizes openness for receiving from the Divine. Folded or palm-to-palm hands represent a prayerful attitude or a beseeching prayer, as do kneeling and gracefully prostrating yourself on the floor. Bouncing, leaping, skipping, and twirling all demonstrate joy. Tears, a bowed head, or motionlessness can each represent sorrow or contriteness. Adding any of these gestures to your dancing can help in expressing your prayers.

The first few times you practice dance prayer on your own, it may be easiest to put on a song with lyrics that express what it is you want to pray. In the instance above, when I feel joyful and grateful, I may put Cat Stevens on the stereo. On the other hand, if I'm feeling a bit melancholy, I will play a song that expresses these emotions more adequately.

However, so long as I choose music that has prerecorded lyrics, I tend to be tied to the words and expressions of the song and my spirit is less free to express its own prayer needs. To allow myself the freedom to pray in a fully spontaneous manner, I prefer instrumentals. Although I try to match tune to mood, sometimes I'll put a collection of instrumentals ranging from classics to blues, soundscapes to jazz and put the CD changer on random play. Then as song turns to song, my spirit, heart, and body can respond as the soul moves me.

Choreographed Dancing

It is well beyond the scope of this book and the breadth of my abilities to try to teach the secrets of great choreographed liturgical dance. However, a few words about choreography may be helpful in your decision of whether or not to go further into the art.

Choreographed liturgical dancing is not quite the same as prayer dancing. Some may say that choreographing your prayer dance takes the soul and spirit out of your offering. But just as there is nothing wrong with reciting a rote prayer, such as the Lord's Prayer, there is nothing wrong with choreographed dance. And just as praying rote prayers on a regular basis, such as praying the Psalms, can enrich your spontaneous praying, so can practicing choreographed dance enrich your spontaneous dancing. However, in both cases, if all you ever do is rote prayer and choreographed prayer dancing, then you are missing the fullness of what each has to offer.

By learning to choreograph your dancing, you are able to add layers of meaning to your prayers. Although there are no standards of meanings for liturgical dance moves, there are common themes throughout. For example, a low sweeping bow implies submission, while raised arms with palms uplifted signifies yearning or desire. Virtually all liturgical dance movements are borrowed from traditional dance forms, including ballet, hula, and modern dance. One trained in liturgical dance takes these moves and choreographs them in order to tell or enhance a story or to kinesthetically express a portion of the worship service. In most cities today there are a number of churches that have liturgical dance troupes, and in virtually every part of the U.S. there are liturgical dance instructors and performers available from whom to learn and with whom to collaborate. There are also resources on the Internet that can help you learn liturgical dance, including an excellent online video-workshop produced by the General Board of Global Ministries of the United Methodist Church (http://gbgm-umc.org/umw/move/). Additionally, liturgical and sacred dance workshops and videos are available throughout the United States

The Heart of Prayer

One might think at this point that the art of dance itself is the focus of prayer dancing, but nothing could be further from the truth. Prayer dancing focuses on communicating to and with God in one of the most intimate forms of expression available. In prayer dancing the whole body is involved in active praying, but for the body to respond, there must be prayer in the heart.

As I ready myself to practice prayer dancing, I often think of Paul's words about prayer and the work of God's Spirit within us:

If we don't know how or what to pray, it doesn't matter. He does our praying in and for us, making prayer out of our wordless sighs, our aching groans. (Rom. 8:26, *The Message*)

More than once when I could not find the words to pray, my movements—with the help of my body and an instrumental piece to match my emotional state—communicated far more than my lips ever could. It's as if the Spirit within me has taken over my body to express my soul's yearnings.

To prepare your own heart for prayer dancing, begin by either choosing and starting your music selections, or focusing on the dance rhythms. Then close your eyes and try to clear your mind of distracting thoughts. Turn your spiritual eyes to God and then begin to "feel" the rhythm. If you're using a song with lyrics, let the words of the song wash over and through you as a prayer. Allow your body to spontaneously move, but continue to center on either the words of the song or the emotions you're expressing. In your inner being, reach out to God with your inner spirit and seek to be open to whatever God may have in mind for you. As you begin to move more spontaneously with the music, try to free your mind from intentional thoughts and allow God's Spirit to move through you and within you, perhaps planting seeds of thought and emotions as the Spirit interacts with you.

On the other hand, prayer dancing is not a mindless proposition. As you pray, take time to intentionally express whatever it is you feel and need. If your prayer is a joyful one, intentionally dance in that manner. If you are dancing to seek guidance, you might dance more pensively than otherwise. In every event, be intentional in making your prayers substantive.

Prayer Dancing Accoutrements

Not much is required to offer your prayers through dance: a willing heart, a bit of space, and the ability to engage in movement. Everything else is optional, including, as I've mentioned, music. However, there are a number of options that can heighten and widen the experience.

Music

As mentioned earlier, music enhances the dance experience. Choose songs with lyrics that characterize the prayer that you want to offer, or instrumentals that resonate with the emotions you are feeling.

Dance Attire

The clothes you choose to wear while dancing can significantly enhance your prayer. For safety and comfort's sake, begin by wearing clothes fitting for the level of physical exercise you will engage in. Footwear that is slip resistant is a necessity, whether you're dancing on your living room rug or hardwood floors. Wearing leggings can help prevent cramps and shin splints. Once you have provided for the safety aspects, there are a variety of dance-specific garments you may choose to wear as you dance. There are many different costumes used by liturgical dance troupes that you may want to purchase, especially if you are going to be dancing at a worship performance in the public's eye. Some may find wearing these costumes reinforces the specific purpose of their prayer. For instance, if your prayer is one of remorse or repentance, wearing a costume reminiscent of sackcloth may help set the tone for the prayer dance.

Ribbons, Streamers, and Flags

These accessories are widely used by liturgical dance troupes. I have had the opportunity to use ribbons a number of times and have found them to add much beauty to my prayers. Although ribbons can be used in spaces as small as a typical living room, you do have to be careful with them—imagine having to explain how the vase of roses broke while you were praying! All three of these accessories are most suitable in larger worship spaces, especially for liturgical dancing; however, ribbons and streamers can also be used effectively for personal worship and prayer in the back or sides of a sanctuary without drawing too much attention. Dance ribbons are wide ribbons about ten feet long attached to a baton. Streamers tend to be a bit shorter, but are significantly wider and may have multiple lengths. They too are attached to a baton. Flags come in a variety of shapes and sizes, but are rather large and usually decorated with a spiritual symbol.

Ribbons and streamers can be used to accentuate dance moves by streaming them with your hands and arms. Longer ribbons and streamers require significant movement across the room to get them to stream behind you, so plan on getting a physical workout as well. If limited space is an issue, simply use a ribbon that is three feet long or shorter—these shortened ribbons can even be effectively used by those restricted to wheelchairs.

To use a ribbon or a streamer in dance, use wide gestures to extend the streaming material—too short of a circle can easily tangle the ribbon or streamer. Waving the material in figure eights and in "S" patterns, as well as any other figure you may choose, can create beautiful patterns in the air.

Flags are more difficult to handle, but can bring a level of majesty often unknown in the church. With practice, liturgical dancers regularly use two flags to create a stunning performance. The sounds of the flags whipping through the air add to the aura of the dance. The basic movement in dancing with flags is to wave them in such a way as to unfurl them and create both a visual and aural sensation. Waving them in basic figure eights, using "S" motions, and twirling them are all common movements.

Once again, don't forget that the purpose of the dance is to focus your heart and mind on your prayers, so once you have mastered a few of the basic movements, let your spirit guide your movements.

AMSLAN: A Supplementary Form of Dance

Although technically not a dance, using American Sign Language to pray in rhythm has become a popular way to add movement to prayer. Although many of us don't "speak"

AMSLAN, it is simple to pick up a few basic words such as *God, Lord, Jesus, Spirit, Soul, Mind, Give, Want, You, Me,* and *I,* and then add them to the dance repertoire. This allows the dancer to add specific thoughts to the prayer, thus allowing the prayer to take on yet another layer of meaning.

There are a number of ways to use signing in prayer dancing. The first, and probably most popular way, is to sign the words of a song that's playing in the background. If your prayer dancing is in a public worship service, know that—whether you are the prayer leader or simply one of the participants—many eyes will be on you. Therefore, it is important to remember that when you dance, especially when using sign language, your *whole* body is a part of your offering, including your facial expressions. We pick up so much from watching facial expressions that you will want to ensure your whole affect matches what you're saying with your hands. As you do, you'll discover that using sign in prayer dancing is one of the most dramatic and moving forms of prayer available to you.

When you sign a song, remember that AMSLAN is a shorthand language. Although some do sign exact English, most of the time signing drops words from most phrases. For instance, if you were to sign, "Come, now is the time to worship," you would only sign the words *Come, Now, Time,* and *Worship.* Not only does this make signing more efficient, it also means you have fewer words to try to remember if you're going to be presenting a song as a prayer.

A second way to use sign in prayer dancing is to sign your response to a song that's playing. This would be similar to punctuating a song with a verbal "Amen," a "Praise the Lord," or a "Yes, God." What you actually would be saying in sign would be totally up to you, your sign vocabulary, and how you were being moved in your spirit. You might offer a complementary prayer in response—for instance, "I come worship" as a response to the song "Come, Now Is the Time to Worship."

A third way to use sign in dancing is to do away with music completely and pray to the natural rhythms around you or in your head. The number of words and phrases you know in sign will determine how you use it in expressing your prayer. Having a limited vocabulary isn't necessarily a hindrance, since prayer dancing is generally used to express emotions rather than intercessions.

Finally, children are naturals when it comes to having an affinity for signing and dance. Most any children's song can be easily translated into sign language using online sign language dictionaries or using a good sign language book such as Lottie L. Reikehof's *Joy of Signing.* By teaching children a song or two in sign, they have the opportunity not only to experience the joy and freedom of adding movement to prayer, but they learn an important communication skill as well. Of course, the same could also be said of those of us who can't sit still.

Learning and and using sign in prayer dancing allows a wider expression of communication in prayer than is possible with dance alone. There are many good resources available online, in most bookstores, and in your public library that will help you learn sign and expand your dancing horizons.

Prayer dancing is one of the most underutilized forms of prayer practiced. Perhaps most of us are simply too self-conscious when it comes to expressions that may call attention to ourselves. However, when we dance in prayer it is important to remember that we are dancing to an audience of one—to the divine presence that certainly can be nothing less than pleased when we pray with our whole selves. Who knows, perhaps our prayers will be better heard when we put our heart, mind, soul, *and* body into the act.

CHAPTER 3

Action Prayer

One of the most powerful prayer experiences I've ever witnessed was an action prayer offered by a twelve-year-old boy at summer camp. The camp staff had agreed that we would test some of the kinesthetic prayers that I was developing for this book, so we introduced them to the children during the final worship activities for the week. The camp was by a lake, and the shore was covered by thousands of round, oval, and flat smooth stones—perfect for skipping and tossing into the lake. Each child was invited to choose up to three of the stones and then to find a place on the shore to sit. We gave each a permanent marker and asked them to think and pray about what it was in their lives that they wanted God to throw out—things like anger, shame, or sickness. Then they were to write on each of the stones a one or two word description of what they wanted God to get rid of. After a few minutes we asked the children to project what they were getting rid of onto the rocks and then to throw them into the lake as far as they could.

The scene that unfolded was inspirational. Some of the children teared up, others expressed relief. But then there was

Teddy. Every camp has a Teddy—the ADHD kid with no medication and no sense of boundaries. Teddy was from a troubled family and he was a troubled child. He didn't respond well to direction, and he didn't often sit still. True to form, he didn't sit still here either. He gathered his stones with some care and he took seriously the effort to write something he wanted to get rid of from his life. One of the counselors was near him as he began to write and to hear him cry, "I don't want to treat my mama like I have been. I want to love my mama." And then he threw the stone as far into the lake as his twelve-year-old arm could muster. When Teddy was finished, he left the prayer time with a new determination to love his mother with his actions, not just his words.

Action prayers are powerful tools in the prayer tool belt.

Prayer in Action

Prayer has long had an action component to it. When someone says, "Let us pray," most of us immediately bow our heads and close our eyes. When we say grace, many of us fold our hands a certain way, or we may reach out and hold the hand of whoever is closest. And let us not forget the positions of prayer: kneeling, lying prostrate, or reaching to the sky with our hands and arms.

Historically, prayer has almost always been embodied in some tangible way. One of the most ancient prayer actions is anointing the head with oil. This practice has been tied to both consecration and healing prayers and is found in a number of cultures. Baptism and ritual washings are other ancient forms of enacted prayer that demonstrate and symbolize, to those watching, the intent of the prayer, as well as serving as a personal testament to the one who is offering the prayer.

Virtually every culture in every age has engaged in some sort of action prayer. For those of us who can't sit still, though, the actions of these prayers are less about being demonstrative to those who might see us, as they are the integral language of prayer itself.

Action Prayers

Although there are literally thousands of different actions that can be attached to prayer, and most are single actions such as kneeling, genuflecting, and bowing, for those who can't sit still, an effective action prayer involves movement that is either continuous or periodic.

Casting Prayers

In the opening paragraphs, I introduced an account of a casting prayer we practiced during summer camp with nine- to twelve-year-olds. I've discovered that this is one of my favorite casting prayer styles.

Casting prayers use projection as their foundation. It's very much like the biblical story of the scapegoat. In Leviticus the high priest was to choose a pair of goats each year to serve as a sacrifice for the nation's sin. The priest sacrificed a bull and one of the goats to cover their sins, and then we read:

> Then Aaron shall lay both his hands on the head of the live goat, and confess over it all the iniquities of the people of Israel, and all their transgressions, all their sins, putting them on the head of the goat, and sending it away into the wilderness by means of someone designated for the task. (Lev. 16:21)

The priest transferred, or projected, the sins of the nation onto the goat and then it was "cast" away into the desert. This is what all casting prayers are about—the transferring of something from our lives onto an object and then casting the object out of our lives in one way or another.

Whenever you're at a time in life when you recognize you're carrying something you need to get rid of, whether that be worry, anxiety, guilt, shame, a bad habit, or whatever else that's chained to your heart, casting prayers can be very effective. Begin by going to that place where you find a sense of peace or empowerment—and where you have enough space to throw a rock really hard. Whether that's a place with water, trees, or the open plains, it's most helpful to be somewhere you feel close to God. If there is a paucity of stones where you're going, you will want to stop by the roadside somewhere along the way to pick up as many as you feel you need.

It's in the search for the right stones that my prayer time actually begins. As you look for your casting stones, take the time to breathe slowly and deeply while your eye scans the ground. Meditate on what it is you are doing, what problem or care you are casting out, and let your heart choose just the right stone. Sometimes I'll choose a smooth stone that's particularly fit for skipping, but sometimes my issue is particularly painful or even a bit ugly so I'll pick a stone that matches. You may want to choose several stones, especially if the issue is complicated or deeply ingrained. Remember, the disciple Peter invariably had to experience something three times before he got it right.

When you've chosen your stones and have arrived at your destination, allow yourself the time and space to get centered. I like to look across the horizon and at the sky while picturing myself in my mind's eye as God might be seeing me. Focus your thoughts on God and roll over in your mind whatever burden you're carrying. Ask God to remove the burden. Then, just like the priest in Leviticus, project whatever burden you're carrying onto the stones in your hands.

If you remembered to bring a marker or something else to write with, you may jot onto the stones a couple of words that sum up the issue. I almost never have a marker when I need it, so I've learned I can project my burdens onto the stones without actually having to write anything on them. On the other hand, you may realize you're missing something spiritually nurturing when you omit this step, so trace the words onto the rocks with your finger as a tactile reminder to yourself and to God.

As you write or trace the issue on the casting stone, speak to God about the issue. Why has this become such a burden to you? If the burden was gone, but the issue was not, what would you do about it? What is your responsibility in the issue, and what is beyond your control? What are you asking God to do in your life? Ponder these questions as you hold or rub the stones in your hands. Try to see the stones as the embodiment of the problem and look at the burden carefully. Are you carrying something you don't need to carry?

Take your time at this point as you look at the casting stones. Try to get to the point where the burden and the stones are one-in-the-same and you know the stones have received your issue. Then, with all your might, throw each stone just as far as you can into the water, down the gully, or across the field, knowing that as you throw it, your burden has been cast out of your life. You might find comfort in the biblical promise that "as far as the east is from the west, / so far he removes our transgressions from us" (Psalm 103:12).

The last part of this action prayer is probably the most important.

> *Pause.*
>> *Feel.*
>>> *Listen.*
>>>> *Wait.*

Pause. Watch the stone fly across the sky and out of sight.

Feel. Allow whatever emotions attached to the prayer wash over you. Are you feeling relief and a sense of freedom? Do you feel a sense of loss? What is your heart feeling?

Listen. What is God saying to you in the sounds all around you and the whispering within you? Is there something you have to do to make the issue right? someone you need to forgive? to confront? to apologize to? What is your spirit saying?

Wait. Don't be in a hurry. This is where most of us who can't sit still have the most difficulty. We threw the rocks, now it's time to go home. But waiting for a few moments to allow the Spirit of God to wash through us is an excellent discipline that even those of us with extra hyperactivity need to practice now and again.

If during this prayer time you realize that the burden hasn't completely gone, don't hesitate to start again. I've had a number of experiences where I had to throw in a *bunch* of rocks before I felt anything like relief. But when I'm consistent in the accompanying prayers, I have almost always discovered a sense of peace that I wouldn't have experienced otherwise.

Variations

There are a couple of quite effective variations I've used in casting prayers over the years. Since the goal of casting prayers is to enact the separation of ourselves from our burdens, any movement prayer that embodies that feeling of separation can be used.

The first variation is "kindled" prayers. This kind of prayer is not as active as casting stones, so it may not be quite as effective for someone who can't sit still, but it definitely has its uses. Instead of just about whatever burden you're carrying, you express it either in writing or in images on a piece of a paper. It might be helpful to use the same meditative questions as in the stone casting exercise, but in any case, the goal is to get the issue down on paper in some way. Once again, do this in a prayerful and listening attitude in order to hear what your spirit and what God may have to say. As you write or express yourself through the arts, try to be as thorough as possible in describing your burden and the circumstances surrounding it. The exercise should be as cathartic as possible in order to cleanse your spirit— honesty is the only policy here, and God can not only "take it," but already knows all about it.

Once your writing or your art is complete, mentally and emotionally transfer the burden from your heart onto the paper. Again, take some time to reread or explore your paper. Then, in a safe receptacle, such as a fireplace, barbecue grill, camp fire pit, or large ashtray, set fire to the paper and watch your burden go up in flame and smoke. As it burns, realize that God is receiving your prayers and your burden. Let it go as the flames and smoke rise into the air. When it has been completely consumed, take a moment to reflect on your prayer time and offer a word of thanks.

The second variation is a sport-driven prayer that a number of my friends might try to use to legitimize their absence from church: the "driving" prayer. This alternative uses all the principles of the stone casting prayer except it uses golf balls and a three, four, or five wood. In this casting prayer, your burden is prayerfully projected onto a golf ball and then it is teed up, addressed, and hopefully whacked with a satisfying swing that puts the ball, burden and all, into the nearest water trap. John Maxwell tells of a time when he used a variation of this. He teed up his ball and gave it a terrific whack. Unfortunately, his ball took a wicked slice into the woods, bounced off a tree, and rolled back onto the tee, stopping just in front of him. He then reached down and picked up the ball, put it in his bag, and said to himself, "Some problems just won't go away." And though his words are true, our problems don't have to be burdens that we carry alone. Casting them onto God can relieve us of our excess baggage.

Caim Prayer

We are indebted to St. Patrick and his devoted Irish followers for caim (circle) prayers. Originally, caim prayers called on the encircling of God's favor around the one who is praying. These prayers were recited aloud, generally each morning before facing the day, while drawing a circle in the air by slowly spinning from east to west. Probably one of the most commonly cited caim prayers is the prayer of the Trinity:

> The Mighty Three,
> My protection be,
> Encircling me,
> O Sacred Three,
> The Mighty Three.

Although this is one of the most common of the caim prayers, a number of others were used by Celtic Christians. You can find many more of them by perusing books on Celtic spirituality and Celtic prayer in your public library.

The Celts were an earthy people who took seriously the interplay between our world and the world of the spirits. Curses and blessings carried real consequences and prayer was taken seriously. The Bible verse, "Whatever you bind on earth will be bound in heaven, and whatever you loose on earth will be loosed in heaven" (Mt. 18:18) was considered to be absolute truth by Celtic Christians, and their prayers and practices reflected this belief.

Today there is a growing awareness and belief that the curtain between the spiritual and us is mighty thin and that prayers such as the caim prayer bear a truth that has long been neglected. The caim prayer calls on the graciousness and power of God for divine protection, comfort, and aid by bidding God to surround us with a spiritual circle that keeps the goodness of God on the inside and anything that might be evil on the outside.

I've found the caim prayer to be a powerful tool in my prayer life and I've used it in a number of ways.

There are no specific instructions as to what you might pray for in a circle prayer, but a modern caim might go like this:

> God, I call on your protection.
> Encircle me by your Spirit;
> Send angels to surround me.
> Keep your comforting presence within;
> Keep all that would attack my spirit without.
> Circle me, Lord, with your watchful eye
> And your loving arms.

First, using the prayer to seek personal protection and divine providence is the most traditional way. Before you begin, you may want to consider what you're about to seek from God. Are you in need of comfort? courage? protection? health? What are you asking God to do within the circle, and what is it you want God to keep outside of the circle?

When you have an idea about what you're praying, then begin by standing and closing your eyes in order to center yourself. Take a couple of deep breaths and listen to your breathing. Raise one or both of your arms to shoulder height, and with your index finger point either toward the heavens or the earth, depending on your personal preference. Then pray a caim of your choosing as you slowly draw a circle of divine protection around you. There is plenty of precedence for beginning and ending the prayer facing east, but a caim isn't a magical incantation that demands it be done "just right" in order for it to be a legitimate prayer. The caim is simply a prayer with an affixed action that ritually enacts what you are praying for. The result of prayer is in the hands of God, not in the "correct" practice of some rite or ritual.

As you pray the caim, see in your mind's eye the boundary of the circle being drawn and the divine protection being afforded. Listen to your heart, to your spirit, and for the whispers of God as you pray. You may choose to complete a single circle, or you may want to complete a second circuit in silence as you prayerfully listen.

A second way to use the caim is when you pray for others, either in their presence or when you are alone. This is a less traditional way of praying the caim, but I've used this action prayer in my own prayer life with very good results.

When you choose to pray a caim over someone else, the basic procedures are similar, except instead of drawing a circle around yourself, you draw a circle around whomever you are praying for. This is very effective when you pray for someone you are with. In these cases, I draw a circle around them, either with my finger above their head or by walking around them as I pray a prayer of protection aloud. Recently I came across a Celtic missal that used a chalice to circle the heads of those being prayed for—a very powerful image indeed. Some people have an aversion to being fussed over and the caim prayer might be a bit much for them. In these cases, when I feel led to pray a caim for them, I will pray the circle prayer, but I will either trace a circle in the air while I imagine the person within it, or else I'll simply imagine them within a circle I draw in my mind. Again, it's the heartfelt prayer that God honors, not the ceremonial rites.

The caim prayer is a powerful action prayer. Some who have prayed the caim have told me that in their minds they see angelic beings surrounding them standing shoulder-to-shoulder, wing-tip-to-wing-tip. The same has been true for those for whom I've prayed—there is an incredible sense of God's presence and providence when the caim is invoked in God's name.

Expressive Prayer

As I said in the first part of this chapter, prayer has always had some kind of action component to it. Expressive prayer simply takes these traditional actions and combines them to make prayer more dynamic for those of us who can't sit still. We can call upon a number of traditional actions: *folded hands, bowing, genuflecting, kneeling, prostration, striking, crossing oneself,* and the *orans*.

Folded Hands

I suspect that folding your hands in prayer came into vogue one evening during dinner when someone's children wouldn't keep their hands to themselves while Grandfather's prayer droned on and on. However it came about, we've been bowing our heads, closing our eyes, and folding our hands for as long as most of us can remember.

If you take the time to think about it, you will realize that there are several different ways to fold your hands. Interlaced fingers, palm-to-palm, and clasped hands.

In addition, you can fold your hands in different ways. You can fold them quietly with no fanfare; you can outstretch your arms and bring them quietly together; you can bring them together with a sharp clap; or you can bring them together as in an Egyptian dance by outstretching your arms from your sides (in the shape of a "T"), then raising them up over your head bringing your palms together, and then lowering them to chest level. You could assign meanings to each of the folded-hand styles in order to make them a meaningful part of your action prayer:

Palm-to-palm: A coming into prayer, centering, focusing
Interlaced fingers: Unity, togetherness, singleness of purpose
Clasped hands: Providence, guidance, security

Bowing

This gesture has long been used to signify reverence or respect. There are two degrees of bowing: a simple bow, and a profound bow. A simple bow is made from the waist, and the torso leans forward from a few inches to an angle of forty-five degrees at the most. By lowering your head and eyes as you make a simple bow, you are offering a sign of your respect. A profound bow is made from the waist until your back is horizontal to the floor or lower. A profound bow suggests absolute obedience and subservience.

Genuflecting

The act of kneeling on one knee as a sign of obedience and servitude is several millennia old and is recorded in both the Old and New Testaments of the Bible.

Kneeling

In the early church, kneeling was symbolic of penance, or sorrow for sin. It was the embodiment of being weighed down by burdens being carried in the heart. When one rose from kneeling, this symbolized forgiveness and release from the weight of sin. Later, kneeling would become an act of humility made before a sovereign or a lord. In time, the church adopted this meaning of kneeling as they prayed before God. Both of these meanings can be used in our action prayers.

Prostration

Lying prostrate on the floor has several possible meanings, whether flat on the floor or kneeling forward with your face to the floor. For one, it is a sign of complete surrender and obedience to God. Secondly, it symbolizes reverence, respect, and awe. And thirdly, it demonstrates an attitude of patient waiting for God, whether for an answer to prayer, or for permission to bring a prayer to a close.

Striking

The gesture of striking is shown by the tax collector in Luke 18:13, who beat his chest as he cried out in prayer, "God, be merciful to me, a sinner." Striking your chest, generally signifies great sorrow and self-recriminations.

Crossing Oneself

The sign of the cross was probably first used as a "secret handshake" between Christians during Roman persecution of the church in the second century. In the Eastern Church the proper finger position on the hand used to make the cross is created by pressing together the fingertips of the thumb and first two fingers of the right hand, representing the Trinity. Then a cross is traced by touching the forehead first, symbolizing the purification of the mind; then the solar plexus, symbolizing the purification of our emotions; then the right shoulder, followed by the left shoulder, symbolizing our strength. The Eastern Church ends with their fingers on the left shoulder over the heart. By tracing the cross this way the action reminds us of the commandment to love God with all our heart, mind, strength, and soul. In the East, crossing yourself then ends with a slight bow to show reverence for the cross. The Roman Catholic Church traces the cross similarly, except that it touches the left shoulder first and ends at the right shoulder and omits the final bow. In each case, tracing the sign of the cross is a reminder of the crucifixion and that Christians pray in the name of Jesus.

The Orans

The orans is a liturgical term that describes the action of outstretching your arms and hands palms up in prayer. In later Christian art, it came to symbolize the intercession of the saints between God and those who were praying. Today, the orans is offered as a way to symbolize our eagerness to receive whatever blessings God has for us.

Offering Expressive Prayers

These are just a few of the many gestures that can be added to our prayers. Others might include cupping your hands to represent a willingness to receive what God is offering, covering your eyes to symbolize grief or sorrow, or raising your hands straight up as a sign of joy.

To offer an expressive prayer is to combine these traditional acts into a prayer filled with movement. In some ways, an expressive prayer is like a dance prayer, except that you don't need to discern a rhythm of anything other than the words you're offering. Once again, as you pray, listen to your heart for God to whisper thoughts of comfort, forgiveness, love, and guidance.

An expressive prayer might look a bit like this:

SIGN OF THE CROSS: Oh God,

ORANS: I lift my heart to you.

GENUFLECT: I need to hear your voice. You know the decision that is before me.

ORANS: I am unsure what you would have me do.

KNEEL: Speak, God, for I am listening.

KNEEL OR LIE PROSTRATE: *Silent listening.*

PALM-TO-PALM HANDS: Thank you for hearing my voice and my heart.

PROFOUND BOW: Amen.

Conclusion

As you can see, there are a variety of action prayers to keep you busy for some time. Action prayers are often the most effective prayer methods to use with children, at least with the younger set. There's little more satisfying than chunking a rock deep into the lake knowing that it's taking some of your anger or frustration into the depths.

But these prayers aren't just for kids. From expressing yourself using sacred gestures to drawing a circle in the sand around one needing divine protection, take the time to experience each one. You will come back again and again to some of them.

CHAPTER 4

The Labyrinth

About fifteen years ago, if you asked somebody what a labyrinth was, you might hear about a Greek myth or maybe something about David Bowie as the Goblin King in some fantasy movie by that name. However, today you can find a labyrinth in nearly every metropolitan area if you're willing to look—and most of them you'll find in churches.

Walking a labyrinth is unlike any other experience I've encountered. The fact is, this book began in a labyrinth. For years, as a person who could not sit still, I envied my wife's deep spiritual walk. Her prayer life was the model of the contemplative and as I watched her pray, my heart desperately desired to be still and sit in the presence of my God—but no matter how hard I'd try to still my body and to focus my mind, in just a matter of minutes I'd be fidgeting.

I happened to hear about labyrinths in a conversation at a conference. I was the pastor of a church with a round sanctuary space and thought a labyrinth would be a perfect addition. It didn't take much to convince the Seattle congregation that this would be a great outreach tool, so we took to designing and installing the labyrinth with excitement. After nine hours of work the labyrinth was ready. We dimmed the lights, put on an instrumental CD, and began to pray and walk.

I noticed something almost right away—my mind was quiet and I could walk the labyrinth without having to think about it. I just put one foot in front of the other and followed the path. The further into the labyrinth I walked, the more clarity I had in my prayer. With each reversal of direction in the path, my spirit felt closer to God. By the time I reached the center of the labyrinth I was able to sit on the floor and pray without fidgeting for longer than I ever had before. I felt centered, at peace, and focused. For the first time in my life I found myself in what I could only describe as a contemplative prayer.

It was with reluctance that I finally stood and followed the path back to the entrance of the labyrinth. But as I slowly finished my pilgrimage, I realized the anxieties I'd brought with me to the pathway had been dissipating into the quietness of the evening. I had discovered something for myself, although I wasn't at all sure exactly what that something was.

Over the next several months I made it a habit to walk the labyrinth at least once a week just to be in the presence of God. And as I spoke to others who walked the labyrinth, they shared similar experiences.

The Amazing Labyrinth

The kind of labyrinth we designed looks a lot like a maze, but it has a significant difference—if you stay on the path, you can't get lost. The path takes you to the center and then takes you back again. There are no wrong turns, no blocked paths, and no decisions about which way to go. This type of labyrinth is pilgrimage friendly—but more about that later.

Up until recently, many, if not most, people in the world of church were of the opinion that incorporating a labyrinth into personal worship was tantamount to dabbling in the occult. These opinions were generally based on insufficient knowledge, but some reached that conclusion because of the earliest history of labyrinths.

Labyrinths were at first simple designs embossed on Grecian pottery, coins, and occasionally on the walls of buildings. They represented the mystical home of the minotaur, the legendary half-man, half-beast who inhabited a winding cave on the isle of Crete. Around 1800 B.C.E., a labyrinth structure was constructed on the island of Crete in the city of Knossos. Although this structure was destroyed in 1500 B.C.E., its famous seven-circuit labyrinth continued to be a popular symbol across the Mediterranean shores. The first Christian labyrinth was constructed in Algeria sometime around the year 350 C.E. Although this kind of labyrinth probably didn't garner widespread popularity for another thousand years, during the thirteenth century several European cathedrals inlaid labyrinths into their floors. The most famous of all these cathedral labyrinths is found in the Chartres Cathedral in France, and is an eleven-circuit labyrinth.

Seven-circuit Labyrinth

Little is known about the European cathedral labyrinths, but at one time they were used as an alternative for those who were unable to make a pilgrimage to the Holy Land because of the Crusades. The Roman Catholic Church authorized those who could not go to Jerusalem to alternatively walk a labyrinth in one of seven cathedrals with labyrinths. For a

Chartres Labyrinth

time, labyrinth walking was quite popular. However, as the Crusades came to an end and the interest in Holy Land pilgrimages waned, labyrinths fell into general disuse.

In the 1990s, Dr. Lauren Artress made a pilgrimage to the Chartres labyrinth. There she rediscovered the spiritual journey that had been traveled by Christians centuries ago. She took her newfound joy to Grace Cathedral in San Francisco, where she served as Canon for Special Ministries and began her own pilgrimage in sharing the wonders of the labyrinth with North American Christians.

Finding a Labyrinth

Since most telephone books somehow miss the labyrinth category, you'll have to choose another way to find a labyrinth. You can call one of the local churches in your community and ask if they have or know of a labyrinth in the area. I suggest calling an Episcopal, Catholic, or Unity Church first, since they have shown the most interest in the labyrinth revival. A second way to find a local labyrinth is to use the online Veriditas Labyrinth Locator at www.veriditas.net. This is currently the most comprehensive listing of labyrinths across the U.S., and they are working on an international locator as well.

If you can't find a local labyrinth, don't despair. You could buy or rent a canvas labyrinth, though this can be rather pricey. Some local rental companies are carrying canvas labyrinths for indoor use, and some companies are willing to ship. An Internet search for "labyrinth rental" or for "labyrinth" and "rent" yields several options (but don't rent the David Bowie movie by mistake). Canvas labyrinths are both beautiful and durable and are very popular in churches that don't want to install a permanent labyrinth, but they can cost thousands of dollars, and they aren't exactly inexpensive to rent, especially if you want the labyrinth for personal use.

I think the best option is to build your own labyrinth. For a mere pittance you can construct a simple three-circuit outdoor labyrinth in as little space as twelve feet by twelve feet, or a more elaborate seven-circuit labyrinth in less than thirty-five feet by thirty-five feet.

Building Your Own Labyrinth

Probably the most difficult part of constructing a labyrinth is deciding which design to use. Many patterns for labyrinths, from the Knossos pattern to Roman patterns, are square. The Internet is a great place to research and find ancient patterns for your labyrinth. Be aware, though, many patterns have been copyrighted, and you will need to get permission to duplicate them. All the patterns in this book are in the public domain, and you are free to replicate them as you'd like.

Size is the next consideration in constructing a labyrinth. To duplicate the Chartres eleven-circuit labyrinth you will need space for a forty-three foot diameter circle, but, for a more modest labyrinth you can get by with as little as a twelve foot diameter circle.

The next decision you will have to make is whether you are constructing a permanent or temporary labyrinth. The difference between permanent or temporary is determined by the materials you build it with. Permanent outdoor labyrinths are often built with stones, bricks, or shells that mark the path. Of course, if you have lots of time, space, and money, you could plant your

Julianna Labyrinth

labyrinth using hedging plants. But if you're like the rest of us, you will probably want to construct your labyrinth in a more economical manner. If you have the time and energy, choosing stones for the paths can be every bit as meaningful as walking the sacred path when it's complete. Know, however, that it takes a *lot* of stones to build a labyrinth. Temporary labyrinths can often be built on public property, such as a park, if you first ask permission. Constructing a temporary labyrinth will take around three hours once you've gathered all the materials, but typically you can remove it in a matter of minutes.

If you are building a permanent labyrinth, the directions that follow will need to be adapted to the pattern you choose; however, the principles are the same.

To build an outdoor, temporary labyrinth you can use a variety of materials, such as spray chalk or marking paint (excellent to use on grassy surfaces—the labyrinth lines disappear after a couple of cuttings), or you can use clothesline, rope, string, twine, or yarn, along with sixteen-penny nails. The directions below outline how to build a temporary seven-circuit labyrinth using nails and yarn—by far the least expensive way to build a labyrinth.

Materials needed: one large skein of yarn, about a hundred and seventy sixteen-penny nails, hammer, scissors, tape measure (optional), fifteen feet or so of string or clothesline, and a printed copy of the Julianna Labyrinth (p. 55). The completed labyrinth will be a little less than thirty feet in diameter.

1. Choose where the center of the labyrinth will be (use the tape measure or the fifteen foot string to ensure you have enough room in all directions for the circuits). Tie the string to a nail and drive the nail into the ground.
2. Tie a knot into the string three feet from the center nail.
3. Measure and tie a knot every eighteen inches from the first knot until you have tied seven more knots (you should now have eight knots, one at three feet and seven at eighteen inch intervals).
4. Decide where the entrance to the labyrinth will be (some put the entrance at the westernmost point so that you enter facing east). Stretch the knotted string out to its fullest extent to the entrance point and pound a nail into the ground next to the eighth knot, leaving at least one inch of the nail exposed—do not attach the knotted string to the nail.

5. Tie one end on the skein of yarn to this nail and take the yarn in one hand and the knotted string in the other. Walk to the opposite side of the labyrinth, unrolling yarn as you do, and place a nail next to the eighth knot, again leaving at least one inch of the nail exposed.

6. Stretch the yarn and attach it to the nail with a knot. Cut the skein loose from the nail. The yarn should stretch from one side of the labyrinth to the other and should pass over the nail in the center.

7. Repeat steps four and five, perpendicular to the center line so that you have a cross in the grass. Eyeball the yarn lines to ensure the labyrinth cross is more like a + than an x and that the cross centers over the nail in the center.

8. Return to the center of the labyrinth. Facing the "back" of the labyrinth, measure nine inches from either side of the center nail on the horizontal cross piece and pound a nail in each place. Attach one end of the yarn to one of the nails and with yarn in hand, walk to the entrance. Measure nine

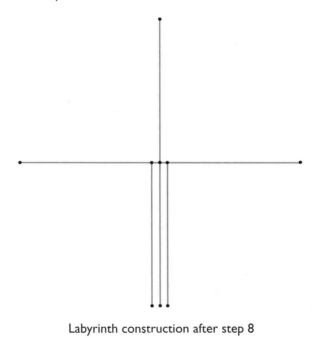

Labyrinth construction after step 8

inches on either side of the vertical cross and pound a nail in each place. Stretch and attach the yarn to one of the nails so that the yarn is parallel to the cross. Cut the yarn and do the same on the other two nails. Your results should be similar to the illustration (p. 57).

9. Next, begin laying out the circuits by attaching one end of the yarn to the leftmost entrance nail. Take the yarn in one hand and the knotted string in the other, take a couple of paces clockwise and pound a nail in at the eighth knot length leaving one inch of the nail exposed. Stretch the yarn from the entrance nail to this one and wrap the yarn around it two or three times and then tap the nail in to just above ground level. Take a few more paces and repeat the process. Make sure you place a nail in the ground at all of the points of the cross as you work your way around. You should use about sixteen nails in the process, though you may choose to use more to make the circuit more circular. When you reach the rightmost entrance nail tie the yarn off and cut it.

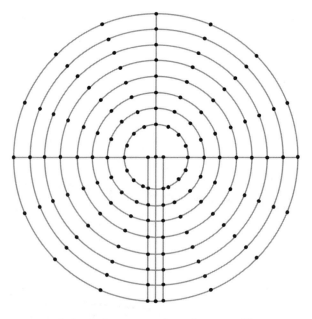

Labyrinth construction after step 10

10. Repeat this process at the seventh knot circuit and on through until you have done the same at the first knot. When you finish, the labyrinth should look similar to the illustration (p. 58).

11. Next, remove the knotted string from the center, wind it up, and save it for the next time. Then begin making the labyrinth paths by removing pieces of yarn at the appropriate places. Begin at the entrance and cut the yarn at the center entrance nail. Then attach each end to one of the "nine inch nails" leaving an eighteen inch entrance. Trim the excess yarn and tap the nail until it is just above ground level. Do the same with the next five yarn circles. (There should be two complete yarn circles when you have finished this step.)

12. Using the printed illustration (p. 60), attach a diagonal from the third yarn circle on the right to the fourth yarn circle on the left. Then remove the section of yarn to that is forming a barrier to the third circuit on the left and the section that forms a barrier to the third circuit on the right. The diagonal yarn should now direct the labyrinth pilgrim from the entrance to the third circuit to the left, so that they will begin walking clockwise.

13. Follow the third circuit to its end at the horizontal cross. Using the printed illustration as a guide, place a nail approximately eighteen inches this side of the cross on the third yarn circle (the yarn circle to your left). Snip the yarn on the third circle and tie the end to the newly added nail, thus leaving a pathway to the left to the second circuit.

14. Using the illustration, snip the yarn at the appropriate places and add nails as needed to create a complete labyrinth. The finished product should look like the illustration.

15. If you accidentally snip the yarn at the wrong place, simply add a piece of yarn to replace it. Again, add nails as needed.

16. To dismantle the labyrinth, remove the nails and the yarn. The yarn is not reusable, but the nails certainly can be if they are cleaned, dried, and stored appropriately.

Finished labyrinth

Walking a Labyrinth

Several practices can enhance your labyrinth prayer time. First is the setting. It is helpful if the setting is peaceful and serene. After building a yarn labyrinth at a camp for older elementary school children, we augmented the atmosphere by recruiting a musical camp counselor to play her flute nearby while the children walked the labyrinth. The melody of the flute, coupled with the sound of songbirds and a breeze rustling through the trees, allowed even the most hyperactive children to find a few moments of peace as they prayed. Incorporating music or luminaries, or placing icons or other symbols along the path, can help create a setting conducive to praying.

When walking a labyrinth that others are also walking labyrinth etiquette is also important. Mostly just keep in mind common courtesy—walk and pray quietly, don't strike up a conversation with someone on the labyrinth, don't run, quietly step into an adjoining circuit to pass others when you need to, and so on. Here is a list of some of the most common courtesies when embarking ona a labyrinth pilgrimage.

Common Courtesy on the Labyrinth Walk

1. Walk, don't run—it's not a race.
2. Walk and pray quietly.
3. If the labyrinth is a carpeted or a canvas labyrinth, it is appropriate to remove your shoes to minimize wear and tear. It is also appropriate to keep your shoes on if you need them for support.
4. Refrain from conversation while in the labyrinth.
5. Refrain from hugs or other physical contact unless previously agreed on.
6. When you encounter someone who has stopped or is walking slower than you, step onto a circuit running alongside yours, pass them, then reenter your circuit to continue.
7. When you meet someone coming toward you on the labyrinth, quietly step off of your circuit to let them pass. It is perfectly all right to greet them with "Peace be with you" or some other quiet blessing.
8. Although it is okay to stop, sit, or kneel in prayer at any corner of the labyrinth, try to do so as unobtrusively as possible.

The Practice of Labyrinth Walking

There's more to walking and praying a labyrinth than strolling merrily along the path. For a meaningful walk, it is important to be intentional about centering, praying, and listening. These three components are often referred to as *Purgation, Illumination,* and *Union,* and they provide the framework for your time in the labyrinth.

People walk and pray labyrinths for various reasons. Some walk to seek wisdom when faced with a decision. Others walk to experience the presence of the holy or to find a spiritual balance in their lives. Still others walk in order to seek healing, be it mental, spiritual, or sometimes even physical.

Whatever brings you to a labyrinth, begin your walk with a time of centering and focusing on the present moment. Many people start their labyrinth walk by kneeling or standing in prayer a few feet in front of the entrance to the labyrinth. During this time it may be helpful to close your eyes and listen to your own breathing. Allow the stillness of your body to quiet your mind as you contemplate beginning your walk.

When you're ready, open your eyes and begin your labyrinth walk. As a personal sign of their devotion to prayer, many people bow to the center—or to the east if the labyrinth faces east—a moment before they take the first step into the labyrinth. As you slowly walk along the path toward the center, allow your thoughts, anxieties, stresses, and worries to slide away with each turn. This process of continuing to center is called *Purgation,* because you are purging your mind and spirit of unhealthy thoughts, concerns, and attitudes.

As you walk toward the center, allow your mind to mull and pray over whatever brings you to your walk. If you have a decision to make, ponder your options and lift them up silently to God. If you are trying to achieve balance in your life, contemplate what is unbalanced and offer that to God. The walk toward the center is about unloading your heart of whatever you're carrying and turning it over to God.

Some who have studied the labyrinth have suggested that a physiological response to labyrinth walking helps the mind to clear itself of negativity. Because the labyrinth changes your direction one-hundred and eighty degrees every so many steps, it is thought that your mind shifts its focus from the left side of your brain to the right and back again with each new turn. Further, since you do not have to consciously make a decision about which way to turn, the brain waves flow freely from side to side without serious interruptions. It is believed that by the time you reach the center of the labyrinth, your mind has found a natural balance in blood flow and synaptic activity. This balance, some suggest, puts you in a place of heightened awareness to your surroundings, and particularly to your spirituality, thus by the time you come to the center of the labyrinth, you are ready to hear from God.

When arriving at the center of the labyrinth, most people sit, kneel, or stand in prayer for a period of time. I personally recommend sitting or kneeling if you can, since time spent in the center is often the most fruitful of the labyrinth walk.

Praying and listening should be your two primary activities in the center. Most people indeed discover that when they've reached this point in their labyrinth walk, they have reached a place of balance and peace that allows them to engage more fully the presence of the Holy. If you have entered the labyrinth in order to make a decision, this is the time to seriously consider your options, and, if a decision is to be made, the center is the place most people find the most appropriate spot for making that decision.

Because the prayer time in the center of the labyrinth is often so powerful, many call this time a period of *Illumination*. Those who seek God intentionally in the center of the labyrinth regularly experience moments of incredible lucidity where they feel the presence of God and discover the answers to whatever they have been seeking.

Once you feel compelled to finish your pilgrimage, turn and begin the journey from the center to the fringes once again. As you walk, take the time to integrate whatever you have experienced into your life. This portion of the labyrinth prayer is traditionally called *Union* because during this time you have the opportunity to unify the experience of your prayer with the rest of your life. If you've made a decision during your walk, this would be your opportunity to consider how you will be integrating that into your life.

I often find that this final stage of the labyrinth walk is sort of like waking up in the morning. With each step I slowly become more aware of my surroundings and my thoughts become more task-oriented. When I have felt God speaking to me, I contemplate what I've heard and what I'll be doing about it.

When you reach the entrance to the labyrinth, many people take one step out of the labyrinth, turn, and bow or kneel in prayer, saying a closing "amen" to what they've just experienced.

At this point, many find it helpful to take a few minutes just to reflect. Some people have special labyrinth journals they use to record their thoughts, prayers, and decisions. Others quietly contemplate what they've just experienced, while some can't wait to tell someone about it. Whatever means you use to process your labyrinth walk, take the time to do so—the process will help seal your walk in your memory for a long time to come.

Enhancements and Alternatives

You can enhance your labyrinth walk in a number of ways, depending on the purpose for the walk. If you are setting up a labyrinth for general prayer, adding candles or luminaries can help create an atmosphere of peace and reverence. Adding icons or other symbols at the labyrs, the 180° "corners" on a labyrinth, can give the pilgrim a cause for pausing and meditating on the object. These symbols don't need to be blatantly religious in nature. Pinecones, shells, leaves, interesting rocks, photographs, and artwork can all be important symbols that inspire deep meaning to those walking and praying. In our church's first labyrinth, one of our members bought a stack of ceramic tiles and painted a word or phrase on each. He used words such as *Imagine* and *Dream*. He also painted "This is my body" and other religious phrases. We would scatter these around at random throughout the labyrinth, and many times people would recount how meaningful these tiles were in helping them focus their prayers.

Another way to enhance the labyrinth experience is to make the pilgrimage in some manner other than by walking. One of the most moving experiences I've watched was a woman who chose to make the trek on her knees. At every corner she stopped and would pray intently before moving again. On the other hand, one of the most fulfilling experiences I had was one evening when the group asked us to play lively praise music over the sound system. We did so and we all discovered the joy of dancing the labyrinth. Together on the labyrinth, and yet each of us on our own, we skipped, twirled, and lightly stepped all the way to the center and back. The sounds of joy and exhilaration were profound as we finished, and the prayers offered were all ones of thanksgiving and gratitude.

There are alternatives to the traditional labyrinth for those who would like a different experience. The most commonly used is the finger labyrinth. A finger labyrinth is a small labyrinth pattern on which you trace the paths with your finger. The Lucca Cathedral, built before the thirteenth century in Italy, has a nineteen-inch labyrinth carved into one of the entrance columns that was probably used as a finger labyrinth by worshipers before they entered. Tracing the pattern with your finger can produce similar experiences to that of walking a labyrinth.

Finger labyrinths can be as simple or as complex as any full-sized labyrinth. You can use any of the patterns in this chapter as a finger labyrinth simply by spreading the book flat and tracing the path with your finger. More elaborate finger labyrinths are available from many sources, including Amazon.com. One of the most popular is *The Sand Labyrinth* by Lauren Artress. This labyrinth is an etched pattern that you sprinkle sand on and then follow the path with your fingertip. *The Sand Labyrinth* has the added bonus of creating multiple tactile sensations at once—your finger feels the roughness of the sand while it traces the labyrinth pattern, a movement that involves the finger and the hand even as it engages the brain on several levels. There are other finger labyrinths made from cloth, ceramic, wood, and virtually every other material imaginable.

Approach using a finger labyrinth the same as if you were about to walk a labyrinth. Take time to focus. Engage in purging your mind as you travel to the center. Pray and listen for illumination in the center. And integrate your experience as you trace the path to the entrance again.

One of the obvious beauties of a finger labyrinth is that it is portable and accessible. Printing out a labyrinth pattern on paper, folding it up, and keeping it in your briefcase or purse allows you to engage in a labyrinth prayer almost anywhere and anytime.

A relatively new labyrinth style has come onto the market called the two-handed labyrinth. These labyrinths are built side-by-side and are mirror images of each other so that when you trace the paths simultaneously you are intensely engaging both sides of the brain. This should have an incredible calming and centering effect on most of us who just can't sit still.

Two-handed Labyrinth

Finally, one of the newest options in labyrinth "walking" is the online labyrinth. I've discovered two of them. The first is connected with Grace Cathedral in San Francisco (www.gracecathedral.org/). This labyrinth offers an opportunity to trace the pattern with an on-screen icon, using your mouse. It also offers a musical accompaniment for the pilgrimage. The second online labyrinth is a presentation by a collaboration of churches and worship groups in England (www.yfc.co.uk/labyrinth/online.html). They have reproduced their labyrinth experience in a highly interactive format that includes music, meditations, and images. However, this labyrinth journey lacks the kinesthetic satisfaction of tracing or walking the pattern itself. On the other hand, their Web site offers a kit for creating their labyrinth pattern and experience in your own community.

Conclusion

The challenge of finding a labyrinth to walk is generally the only drawback to giving this exercise a try. However, those who have made the effort report that the times they spent walking their labyrinths were some of the most fruitful and satisfying prayer times they've ever spent. Indeed, this reflects my own experience, and I've been scoping out a section of my front yard for a small, three-circuit labyrinth. You may find yourself doing the same once you've practiced this exercise.

CHAPTER 5

Prayer Beads, Daisy Chains, & Counting Prayers

Counting your blessings, for those of us who can't sit still, is tantamount to counting sheep. Sleep or distraction will be the amen to those prayers. And yet, counting prayers using prayer beads or some other kinesthetic means are effective tools to have in the prayer tool chest. We'll explore a number of these tools in this chapter, including prayer beads, "daisy" chains, and finger prayers.

The first time I used prayer beads was when my wife and I made a "pilgrimage" to Nancy Fowler's farm in Conyers, Georgia. Back in the late eighties and early nineties, a woman in rural Georgia reportedly began seeing visions of the Virgin Mary on the thirteenth of each month. This phenomenon was widely reported, and by 1991 there were as many as 25,000 people visiting the farm on the apparition days. Because we lived nearby, we went a couple of times for curiosity's sake. During one particular visit, thousands and thousands of people were in group prayer, praying the rosary in unison. Actually, "in unison" is misleading, since we were sitting in a group that represented at least five different languages, and all the people were praying in their native tongues. We were each given a rosary and invited to pray aloud. I didn't know the *Hail Mary*, but I chimed in with the *Lord's Prayer* whenever the group prayed it. As I prayed, I noticed that the tactile feel of the beads passing through my fingers helped me to focus on my prayers. In years to come, I would discover new and more relative prayers to use with the beads, but that first experience has stayed with me for years.

Prayer Beads

Probably the most commonly recognized prayer beads are what are commonly called rosaries. The word *rosary* comes from the Latin word for rose garden, but probably was offhandedly used to describe a bouquet of roses. The word entered the common vernacular to describe a collection of writings, particularly anthologies. However, eventually it came to be associated primarily with the collection of prayers or their associated prayer beads.

Typically when we think of rosaries, we think of the Roman Catholic Church's *Hail Marys* and *Our Fathers* (the Catholic version of the *Lord's Prayer*), as well as the common prayer beads used to "count" the rosary. However, prayer beads predate the Catholic rosary by centuries.

No one seems to be certain when the practice of repeated prayers began, but evidence suggests that Hindus were using prayer beads at least a century before the advent of Christ. Hindu devotees would repeat the names of their Dieties as each bead passed through their fingers.

The first use of prayer beads in a manner we would recognize may have been by Buddhists, perhaps as early as 500 B.C.E. It is said that the devotees would pray, "Hail to the Buddha, the law, and the congregation," two thousand times each day. To keep track of these prayers, one hundred and eight prayer beads were carved from the Bodhi Tree and threaded onto a string. (One hundred and eight was the number of the desires one needed to overcome to reach Enlightenment.) After each prayer was said, one bead would pass between their fingers until they had completed the prayer cycle.

In Christianity, the monastic community began praying the Psalms repeatedly as a spiritual discipline. They divided the Psalter into three sections of fifty psalms each and would then pray a section of the psalms on a variety of occasions. For instance, when a priest died, each monk was to pray fifty psalms. If a patron died, they were required to pray two "fifties." It is said that when St. Patrick and his followers would pray the Psalms, they would recite the first fifty and then stand barefoot in a bucket of cold water for the next fifty in order to stay awake. However, the devotion to praying psalms meant that only the literate were able to adhere to this discipline, so the monastics adopted simple prayers to use for their devotions. The *Our Father* prayer was popular, as was the *Hail Mary*. These would be offered once in place of each of the one hundred and fifty psalms.

In the Coptic and Palestinian deserts, the monastics developed a short prayer that combined the invocation of Jesus' name with the mercy prayer: "Lord Jesus Christ, Son of God, have mercy on me, a sinner." This prayer was repeated as many as twelve thousand times each day in order to obey literally the Pauline command to "pray without ceasing" (1 Thess. 5:17). The monastics used prayer beads or knotted cords to help keep track of the prayers.

By the beginning of the second millennium C.E., prayer beads were commonly used by clergy, monastics, and laity alike. Lady Godiva, of coiffeur fame, asked that a string of her personal prayer beads be placed at the foot of a sculpture of Mary. Indeed, the use of prayer beads was so common that the English word we use for bead is a derivative from the Old Saxon *bede,* which means prayer.

Today, the most common Roman Catholic rosaries are made like a necklace with five "decades" of beads; that is, sets of ten beads separated by a larger bead. At the beginning of the circle of beads is a crucifix.

Praying the full Roman Catholic rosary includes reciting and praying multiple times the *Apostles' Creed,* the *Our Father,* the *Gloria Patri,* and a number of *Hail Marys.* (Text to these prayers can be found in any Roman Catholic devotional book or at www.rosary-center.org.) It also includes a time of reflection on the twenty mysteries, which recite the entire story of salvation from the annunciation to Mary, through the crucifixion and resurrection of Christ, to the assumption of Mary. Praying the full rosary consists of praying four times around the beads, with the large beads each representing one of the mysteries. Most folks praying the Catholic rosary pray only one time around the beads and pray a different set of mysteries each time.

Today, however, prayer beads are not limited to the Roman Catholics ritual of praying the rosary. Indeed, many prayer disciplines have adopted the use of prayer beads and have created their own rituals so that everyone can use this effective prayer tool.

Praying a Rosary—Repetitive Prayer

Especially for folks who can't sit still, using prayer beads can be a powerful way to pray. The tactile feel of the beads between the fingers helps to focus the mind by providing an external outlet for the body. It has been said that we can concentrate on only one task at a time, but those of us who can't sit still recognize that we often concentrate best when we project potential distractions into some repetitive movement—it's why many of us bounce our knee while otherwise "sitting still."

There are several ways to use prayer beads. The most common, of course, is the Roman Catholic rosary. However, many Protestants take exception to the veneration of Mary. Also, those of us who can't sit still may find that repetitive prayers are less than helpful, since we may quickly become distracted and abandon these prayers as fruitless.

On the other hand, one of the most helpful disciplines to overcome this "restlessness" is to practice sitting still for increased periods of time, and praying a rosary can aid in that endeavor. Alternatives for using prayer beads without using repetitive prayers follows the next section.

As I've said, there are a number of alternatives to the Roman Catholic rosary; however, the most commonly available string of prayer beads is the Catholic rosary. The following suggestion adopts these beads as the starting point. (Homemade rosaries that use different numbers and prayer options are offered later.)

The Jesus Rosary

CRUCIFIX—*Centering Prayer:* To pray using common rosary beads, begin at the crucifix. Take a few moments to center and focus on the crucifixion of Jesus.

BEAD 1—*Apostles' Creed:* Next there is a single bead. Pray the *Apostles' Creed* here. If you happen to be of a non-creedal church, carefully read the creed to see if there are any statements you cannot embrace and, if so, leave them out. The creed in this instance is used as a testament and a memorial to your beliefs rather than as an assertion to a particular denomination or faith.

TRINITY BEADS—*In the name of:* Following this bead is a gap in the string and then three beads close together. These beads can represent each person of the Trinity, so with each bead offer your prayers in the name of the Father, the Son, and the Holy Spirit.

BEAD 5—*Our Father:* At the next bead pray the *Our Father.*

INVITATORY BEAD—*Invitation:* The next bead is the Invitatory bead. Here pray a simple invocation or invitation prayer asking God to be with you as you pray.

DECADE BEADS—*Jesus Prayer:* The rest of the rosary is five series of ten beads, each series separated by a single bead. For each of the ten beads pray the *Jesus Prayer:* "Lord Jesus Christ, Son of God, have mercy on me, a sinner." A shortened Greek form of this prayer is *Kyrie Eleison,* which literally means "Lord have mercy."

DIVISION BEADS—*Our Father:* After you have prayed a decade (ten beads), pray the *Our Father* at the larger division bead. When you come full circle and reach the Invitatory bead again, say the *Our Father.*

BEAD 5—*Apostles' Creed:* You may then either continue around again for another five decades, or you may begin closing your prayer time by moving toward the crucifix. At the fifth bead (the end bead on the crucifix string), pray the *Apostles' Creed* again.

TRINITY BEADS—*In the name of:* With the Trinity beads, offer your prayer time in the name of the Father, Son, and Holy Spirit.

BEAD 1—*Our Father:* Repeat the *Our Father* at the next bead.

CRUCIFIX—*Jesus Prayer:* Close with the *Jesus Prayer* at the **crucifix.**

Most adults who can't sit still can learn to pray through the rosary at least through one round. In so doing, we are improving our own self-discipline and giving ourselves the opportunity to expand our prayer horizons.

Praying a Non-Repetitive Rosary

Praying repetitively is a great practice for developing self-discipline in our prayer lives. The act of repeating a prayer helps us to focus, and perhaps even to reform, our deepest subconsciousness—which might be a good thing for most of us. However, repetitive prayer should not become the primary method of our praying, lest our prayers become vain repetitions that mean little to us or to God. Using prayer beads to pray more consciously and intentionally is a habit that can have a significant impact upon our spiritual lives.

Once again, you can use the Roman Catholic rosary beads as your prayer tool; however, there are other prayer beads available or you can also construct your own. We'll deal with personal prayer beads in the next section.

If you are using common rosary beads, once again start at the crucifix. Begin your prayer time by thinking about God and God's commitment to you. At the first bead, take time to center through deep breathing. Take a few deep and slow breaths and concentrate your listening on your breathing as you inhale and exhale. The series of three beads will symbolize the fullness of you. The first of these three reminds you to still your mind. Try to become aware of what you are thinking about and then let it go. It might be helpful to visualize putting your thoughts, one at a time, into a jar and placing the jar on a shelf in your mind. Remind yourself that you can always go back later and take up those thoughts again. The second bead is the spirit bead. This bead symbolizes the seat of your emotions. Become conscious of what you are feeling emotionally as you begin this prayer time. If there are negative feelings within—such as anger, frustration, or fear—turn these over to God as you pray. Try to visualize yourself gathering up these feelings in your hands and lifting them up to the light of God. When you have calmed your spirit, it is time to relax your body. The third bead reminds you to become aware of your body. Most of us who cannot sit still are hyper-attentive to our bodies while paradoxically unaware of what our body might be feeling. Take a few moments to check out your body tension. Relax your face muscles, your back, legs, fingers, toes, and so on. Some people begin with the toes and tense them for a moment and then relax them. Then they tense their calves and relax them. They move up from there until they reach their eyebrows, forehead, and scalp. Once they've relaxed their whole body, they often visualize a plug being pulled from the bottoms of their feet and feel their tensions flow out from head to toe. However you choose to relax your body, take a few moments to do so before moving on to the next bead.

The final bead of the crucifix strand is the bead of holiness. At this bead, take time to focus your complete attention on the holiness of God. You might want to visualize a pure, warm, and radiant light emanating from the heavens, or the sound of an angelic choir singing of God's goodness. As you contemplate this holiness, remember that you are a child of God and as such are invited to come into the Divine's presence.

There are five decades of beads on the common rosary. Perhaps not coincidentally, the Protestant *Lord's Prayer* (the *Our Father* with "thine is the kingdom, power, and glory forever" added at the end) can be divided into five parts. Use each of these decades to concentrate on one part of the *Lord's Prayer.*

Here, the Invitatory bead corresponds to the first part: "Our Father, who art in heaven. Hallowed be thy name." This part of the prayer recognizes that God is God, and we are not. Use this decade as a time of praise and recognition of God. For each of the next ten beads, pray a sentence that recognizes God's Godness. Your prayers might include words of praise for what God has done for you—for your life and the blessings you've experienced. They might include words of gratitude, or simply a recitation of God's attributes: "God, you are holy. You are all-powerful. You are the Creator," and so on.

The first division bead calls us to pray: "Thy kingdom come, thy will be done on earth as it is in heaven." This decade includes ten prayers for our "kingdoms." You may want to pray for your nation's leaders here, and this also is a good time to pray for your employer and your pastor. However, besides praying for those in our kingdoms, this is also the time to pray about God's will for you, especially in any decisions you may be facing. Pray about your plans and your future at this time.

The second division bead reminds us to pray: "Give us this day our daily bread." This decade of prayer is a reminder that we are all dependent on the Divine for so much. These ten prayers can include whatever needs you have, as well as remembering to offer thanks for what you have received.

The third division bead: "Forgive us our trespasses as we forgive those who trespass against us. And lead us not into temptation, but deliver us from evil." The next ten prayers could be called the sorrowful prayers, since they recognize our own shortcomings, mistakes, and sin. Confession is the first step to recovery, whether from substance abuse or other sins. Repentance is not doing "it" again, whatever sin "it" is. Take the time not only to acknowledge your lack of perfection, but to use a few of the ten prayers to ask God to guide you *around* the temptations instead of through them.

The final division bead is for a prayer of surrender: "For thine is the kingdom, and the power, and the glory forever." This decade is for all those issues about which we need to pray and to let go and let God. Each prayer recognizes that this is God's world, we are God's creation, and that the Divine has some sort of a plan for us. We are controllers at heart, but as virtually every world faith teaches, our lives are but breaths in the winds of eternity. Use these ten prayers to put God in control of your life. Consider surrendering your ego, your will, your time, your talents, and so on, so that God can make the most out of the life God created.

When you have finished the final decade, you have reached the crucifix strand again, and it is time to begin your amen. At the large bead, pray the *Lord's Prayer* as a whole prayer. At the first single bead, renew your commitment to follow through on the prayers you just completed. Then, with the next three beads, give thanks to the Father, Son, and Holy Spirit. The last single bead is to remind you to take a few moments of silence to listen to what God has to say to you. Finish the prayer at the crucifix and offer the great amen in the name of Jesus.

Personalized Prayer Beads

There are many different kinds and styles of prayer beads. Although the Roman Catholic rosaries are the most commonly available, other faiths and denominations use prayer beads and have developed their own rosaries. These different styles can be found in numerous religious stores and on the Internet. However, perhaps the most satisfying option is to make your own.

To make your own rosary, consider the symbolism of the numbers. For instance, the Anglican prayer beads begin with a crucifix or other religious symbol that is followed by an Invitatory bead. The circle of beads is in four series of seven beads each, with each separated by a division bead. There are thirty-three beads in total on the rosary, representing the number of years Jesus was on earth. The seven-bead series represent the seven days of creation, a single week, and in Hebrew the number seven symbolizes complete wholeness. The four division beads represent the four points of the cross, the four points of the compass, the four seasons, and the four gospels.

Additionally, the color and even the shape of beads can be helpful in your prayers. Red symbolizes sacrifice; blue and purple royalty; black darkness, sin, or evil. Green can represent growth. Yellow can stand for joy. A triangle can represent the Trinity. A circle can represent completeness. A square can stand for truth, the four corners of the earth, or the foundation stone. And so on. What each color, shape, and even number symbolizes is really up to you. The beads you choose should be a doorway into the spiritual realm of prayer.

Before you make your own prayer beads, you will want to have some idea of how you will be praying them. If you will be using your beads for repetitive praying, consider what prayers you will be using. For those planning to pray the *Jesus Prayer* repetitively, an unlooped double strand of ten beads each might be helpful to keep track of the large numbers of repetition. For example, use one strand of ten to count individual prayers, and the other strand for each ten prayers. If you will be praying non-repetitive prayers, consider how you would like to divide your prayer time. The *Lord's Prayer* naturally divides into five or eight parts conveniently. Other prayer types include the ACTS prayer, which divides prayer into Adoration, Confession,

Thanksgiving, and Supplication (asking). Thinking through how you would like to use your beads can add new meaning to your prayer life.

"Daisy" Chains

When America was more agrarian, daisy chains were a common childhood, though sometimes a not-so-*childish,* activity. Daisies' long, fibrous stems can make an elegant, rather simple, chain of flowers. These were regularly worn by children as necklaces or like halos and crowns upon their heads. Unfortunately, as the "simple life" became less simple (probably by the adoption of all those "time-saving devices"), hours spent in quiet reflection and concentration making daisy chains were viewed as a waste of time, and the phrase "making daisy chains" became a term of derision.

However, for those of us who can't sit still, making daisy chains—whether of daisies, dandelions, gum wrappers, paper strips, or paper clips—can be an extraordinary prayer opportunity, an opportunity that lifts not only ourselves but those around us and leaves us with physical evidence of our prayer time. This is an important aspect for those of us who are task-oriented and have a need to see some sort of product for time spent.

Praying daisy chains is a leisurely, and yet rather intense, activity. There are a couple of ways to enter into this prayer time. The first is to gather the materials you will be using to make your chain. If this will be an indoor activity, one of the best prayer chains is made with paper strips. The easiest way is to cut a piece of 8 x 11" copy paper or construction paper widthwise into one-inch strips. You will also need a glue stick or a roll of transparent tape and a pen, pencil, or crayon(s).

To begin your indoor prayer chain, find a quiet place and get yourself centered by closing your eyes and taking a few deep breaths. Listen to your breathing and concentrate, trying to hear your heartbeat. Offer a few words to God to dedicate the prayer time and then take a moment to just relax and listen. When you feel centered, begin your prayer chain by taking one of the strips of paper and writing a prayer note on it. You may simply want to write the name of a person for whom you're praying, or a few words expressing your gratitude or a need. As you write the prayer, offer a few quiet words to God about it. Listen to your spirit to hear if God has some thought or word for you. When you feel ready to close this prayer, form a paper link by bending the paper strip end-to-end and taping or gluing the ends together. Next take another strip of paper and add your prayer to it. Repeat the process, except when you're ready to close the prayer, thread the new paper strip through the previous link, and tape or glue the ends together, forming the second link of the prayer. Continue praying this way until you have exhausted your prayer thoughts. Then, with a last strip of paper, close the prayer time by offering thanks to God and using it to attach the end links of the prayer chain together, thus closing the prayer chain. You can, of course, leave the end links unattached in order to lengthen the chain the next time you pray. If you would like, date and keep your prayer chain somewhere for later reflection.

Making Daisy Chains from Blooming Flowers

As I wrote this chapter, it came to my attention that the art of daisy chain making has been lost to many of us. It's an art that sorely needs to be relearned by our children—and perhaps by each of us.

If you will be praying outdoors, and the flowers are in bloom, consider making a real daisy chain. Almost any blooming flower can be used, from roses to dandelions, but be sure to use flowers that are not endangered (or in your neighbor's garden).

Daisy chains can be made into necklaces, belts, anklets, chokers, or halos.

To make a daisy chain:

Select flowers for the chain. To make a long daisy chain for a necklace or belt, pick the flower stem near the root. You will want a long stem, if possible. To make a halo the flowers should be closer together, so you need less stem length.

Split end of stem. Toward the end of the stem, but not *too* close to the end, split the stem with your fingernail, or carefully with a knife if you're using a woody flower such as a rose. (When making a halo, split the stem closer to the flower as you thread them together.)

Thread flowers together. Slip the stem of the second flower through the split and thread it through until flower meets the stem. Repeat the process of splitting the stem with this second flower, insert a *third* flower through that split, and so on.

Close the loop. To close the loop, make the last split large enough in the stem to thread the first bloom of the chain through it.

If you have flowers in your own yard, or if you have access to a meadow (perhaps in a park), one of the most fulfilling prayer times is to spend your time mindfully walking, picking the flowers as you go, and making the daisy chain as you step from flower to flower. This prayer time is similar to the paper chain prayer above, except as you choose and pick each flower, project a prayer onto it and offer it to God. If you walk slowly and prayerfully as you add each link (each flower) to the chain, you will find yourself contemplating deeply on the person you're praying for, or on the need you're praying about. Again, listen for the Spirit to whisper to your heart as you pray. God often speaks to a quiet heart and mind. When you feel at case about your prayer, often called "feeling released," prayerfully walk to your next flower, pick it, and then pray using it as a focusing tool. Once you are released, add it to your chain. Continue in prayer until you run out of time, daisies (or dandelions), or prayers. It is considered bad form at best and illegal at worst to pick flowers from a public, state, or federal park. Consider using finger prayers or another prayer option when visiting these pubic domains.

Finger Prayers

Finger prayers are the simplest form of counting prayers, although they are by no means insignificant. These prayers are simplest because they take absolutely no preparation or materials. They are significant because they can lead us into a deep, meaningful prayer time.

The five-finger prayer assigns meaning to each of your fingers. The thumb is closest to your heart. Begin your prayer time by centering your heart and then praying for those who are closest to you. These would be your family and your friends. The index finger, also called the pointer, is the finger that represents teaching. Pray then for those who teach and for those who heal. You might remember to pray for your pastor, your teachers (both present and past), as well as those who practice the healing arts. At this point you might also want to lift up those who are ill. The middle finger is the tallest finger and reminds us of our leaders. Pray for your civic leaders (both local and national), world leaders, religious leaders, and your employer and supervisor. The ring finger is the weakest finger of them all. This should remind us to pray for those who are weak, oppressed, in trouble, and in pain. The little finger serves to remind us of ourselves and our rightful place in the universe. Virtually every faith's sacred writings teach that serving others is the mark of righteousness, goodness, and holiness. Pray then lastly for your own needs and desires. (Similarly, finger prayers can also be used to represent the five-part *Lord's Prayer*.)

Kinesthetically, finger prayers may be the least helpful of all the counting prayers, since the fingers serve primarily as symbols and leave us with little to do. However, as the chapter on sensing prayers will introduce, prayer using our bodies can be as kinesthetically helpful as any other tactile-laden prayer type.

Counting prayers, whether using prayer beads, daisy chains, or some other method, work for those of us who can't sit still because they provide both a tactile sensation to our prayers as well as giving us an opportunity to combine motion with meditation. These beads, chains, and counters can be more than just tools to enhance your prayer life; many are also works of beauty. Whether you purchase prayer beads or string your own, the serenity and focus they give can deepen your prayer life significantly.

CHAPTER 6

Sensational Prayer

According to the ADD (Attention Deficit Disorder) Association, somewhere in the neighborhood of fourteen million adults have ADD, half of whom are undiagnosed. That's a lot of people who can't sit still because of their genetics. Of these, many are plagued with what is known as either hyper-tactile sensitivity or sensory defensiveness, medical terms for the "tags in the back of my shirts [skirts, pants, underwear] drive me batty" syndrome. In other words, many of us are super-sensitive to touch. A friend of mine has to buy socks with no seams across the toes because she can feel the seams and they literally hurt. My parents tell me that the pressure on my finger of flipping a light switch on was too much for me until after I was three years old. People who are sensory defensive have less tolerance for pain because they feel things more intensely than the rest of the population. It also means that the right kind of touch can be especially appreciated.

The result is that sensational prayer can have extra potential for us. Because we self-moderate the level of pressure we apply as we pray, we may be able to reach near hypnotic levels of meditation and even approach a contemplative state.

Most kinesthetic prayer methods have to do with using either major motor skills, such as walking and dancing, or object manipulation, such as using prayer beads or casting stones. However, sensational prayer uses neither, making it unique among the kinesthetic prayers in this book.

Sensational prayer uses the body itself as the kinesthetic focus for praying. By directing our kinesthetic focus to a single point of the body, we are often able to free our minds for effective prayer.

The roots of sensational prayer are found in the ancient Asian studies of the body. The discovery that applying pressure to one point on the body effects other parts led to the practice of acupuncture and acupressure. Maps were made of the body's pressure points and the organs and muscles they were connected to. These ancient maps have received a few contemporary updates, but most of the points remain unchanged. Only in the recent past has Western medicine begun to recognize the benefits of this ancient physiological science, and today it is not uncommon to find medical offices devoted to these alternative practices located in a city's mainstream medical arts building.

But sensational prayer has a second parentage as well. Bioenergetic therapy, sometimes referred to as body memory therapy, has received much attention over the past fifty years or so. Bioenergetic therapy depends on pressure and massage of certain points in the body to achieve psychological results. The field of bioenergetics claims that the brain is not the only physical location where memory resides. Instead, memories can be "stored" in any muscle, organ, or tissue of the body, because all body tissue is composed of similar molecular elements, the main element being water. Typically, according to bioenergetic therapists, memories held outside of the brain are negative memories too intense for the mind to fully grasp. These memories create tension and tightness within the muscle and organ tissues, which may promote not only fatigue, but, ultimately, disease. Bioenergetic therapists combine traditional psychotherapies with massage therapy to discover and release these memories.

The point of all this is that self-stimulation and massage can have physiological as well as psychological effects, which is the basis for the effectiveness of sensational prayer.

Sensational Prayer

There are a number of ways to practice sensational prayer. The first is called *directed sensational prayer*. In this prayer style you choose the parts of the body to massage and also what each part signifies to you. The second method is called *pointed prayer* because you massage specified pressure points in order to accomplish multiple purposes, such as prayer and increased concentration. The third is called *memory prayer*, because you massage specific areas of the body in order to relieve stress and tension that may be locked up within your body's memory. These last two methods of praying might be considered a bit unorthodox because of their therapeutic roots. However, each of these prayer styles has the potential to deepen your prayer life significantly as you practice them.

Directed Sensational Prayer

Directed sensational prayer is probably the most orthodox style of the three. As I mentioned in the action prayer chapter, movement and posture have long been a part of prayer. Directed sensational prayer takes action prayer seriously and adds to it a self-awareness component.

When you pray using this technique, the points of your body that you massage are chosen because of their associated meaning to you. For instance, if you are praying with the intention of listening to God, you might choose to roll your earlobe between your fingers. If your prayer has to do with making a decision, you may massage your fingers or hands. These massage points have little to do with manipulating pressure points, but much to do with channeling your prayer focus.

To use directed sensational prayer, it is helpful if you know the purpose of your praying. Sensational prayer is probably not terribly helpful to use as your morning devotional prayer style because you will want to choose your massage point (or points) based on what you hope to accomplish in your prayer time. Once you have decided what you're going to pray, you will need to choose a body part that relates to your prayer. Probably the only restrictions on what part of your body you massage are based on a sense of public decency. You probably won't want to take your socks and shoes off at Starbucks to massage your toes as you pray. On the other hand, you may be perfectly comfortable massaging your hands or your forehead almost anywhere.

Begin your prayer time by getting comfortable. Because sensational prayer can lead to deep meditation, you may want to choose a place to pray that is quiet and secluded, with few distractions. Turn off the phone, the television, and the radio, and though some are aided by quiet instrumental music playing in the background, I suggest that you initially try sensational praying in near silence in order to give your full attention to the task at hand. Besides, if the CD skips or the MP3 tracks come to an end, you may be roused from your prayer time earlier than you would have wanted. Indeed, plan on allowing yourself plenty of time just in case you reach the deep prayer place you're seeking.

Close your eyes and center your mind. Deep breathing exercises are helpful in this endeavor. Intently listen to your breathing as you relax and clear your mind of as many conscious thoughts as you can. When you've centered yourself, begin massaging the part of your body that most directly represents what you hope to accomplish in your praying.

This is not the time for a deep body massage, but a gentle touch that signals your mind to focus on the sensation. As you apply the massage, a part of your mind will remain focused there. You may find that adjusting the pressure slightly in intervals helps you to maintain focus better than an unchanging touch. Continue the massaging motion as you turn your focus to the Divine.

At first you may find it difficult to maintain your massaging motion while you turn your mind to God; however, with some diligence you will find that your fingers, thumb, or palm will continue to move intuitively. As you begin to turn your conscious focus from touch to your prayers, allow your mind to offer its prayer needs without over-managing it. This isn't meant to allow your Freudian "id" to take over, but it is an opportunity to allow your deepest spirit to express itself. Our innermost spirit seldom gets an opportunity to cry out to God with unbridled passion, so if the occasion presents itself, encourage the prayer.

As you pray, try to allow the massage sensation to focus your autonomic and subconscious systems, as well as your conscious mind, on your spiritual prayer journey. You may discover, as you pray, that your prayers become less "word" focused and more "image" based. On numerous occasions I have discovered that my conscious mind begins to focus on what looks like a field of stars all around me. When this happens, I regularly find the stars moving past me and I have a distinct feeling that I have moved into a physical presence with the Divine. In these places, I discover I lose track of time and can spend many minutes sitting in God's presence and just "being." My prayers often lose their sense of form, but I recognize that my well-composed prayers have little meaning when I'm in this "mode."

Directed sensational prayer depends on massage to focus the mind away from other external distractions. Because the massage's pressure is repetitive and gentle, the prayer can have an almost hypnotic effect that can introduce meditative prayer even to those who can hardly sit still at all.

Pointed Prayer for Healing

Pointed prayer for healing combines the ancient practice of acupressure with the power of prayer. Because the kinesthete is so sensitive to touch, the combination of stimulating key pressure points while simultaneously praying can yield satisfying results, and, once again, take your prayer to a deeply spiritual level.

Pointed prayer for healing is particularly effective when it comes to dealing with inner turmoil, distress, anxiety, or melancholy, although many report physical relief as well.

The basics of acupressure are the foundation of pointed prayer for healing. The ancient Chinese developed acupressure from their observations that pressure applied to a given point in the body seemed to create relief of certain symptoms at other points of the body. Over time, they created a map of these pressure points and the arts of acupuncture and acupressure were born. In more recent years, researchers have identified fifteen acupressure points that seem to help in the relief of emotional distress.

There are literally hundreds of acupressure points, each with healing properties for various parts of the body. There are many books and Web sites available to you if you want to explore further. For a complete acupuncture/acupressure chart and related symptom relief, visit www.acuxo.com. Also see J. V. Cerney, *Acupuncture without Needles: Do-It-Yourself Acupressure—The Simple, At-Home Treatment for Lasting Relief from Pain* (New Jersey: Prentice-Hall, 1974). However, for our purposes we will look only at the key points on the hands and the face, since these acupressure points are easily identifiable and accessible.

To practice acupressure, identify the point from the illustrations that you want to stimulate and locate that point on your own body. Then with a thumb or finger, apply pressure to the point by massaging it either in small, spiraling circles, or with a steady, gentle pressure. Practitioners suggest that pressure should be applied between seven seconds and one minute, but gentle pressure over a longer period of time is harmless and doesn't seem to either increase or diminish the desired effects.

Once you've decided which pressure point(s) to massage, you are ready to begin pointed prayer. Begin by locating the pressure point on your hand or head and begin to very gently massage the point. Then close your eyes and begin to center

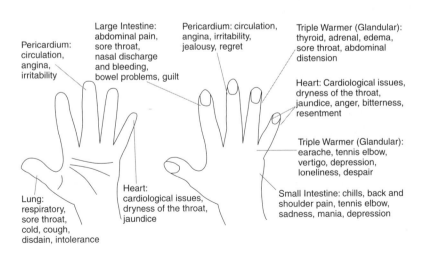

Bowel: sinus inflammation, sneezing, anger, manic behavior, bitterness

Stomach: headaches, eye strain, anxiety, deprivation

Gallbladder: melancholy, sadness, insomnia, rage

Small Intestine: lower abdomen pain, sore throat, hearing problems, depression

Stomach: hunger control, fever, sinus problems, stress, worry, irritability

Large Intestine: abdominal pain, sore throat, runny nose

Central Vessel: teeth and gum pain, depression, mania, shame

Acupressure Points

Although there are hundreds of acupressure points, I have focused on the head and hands because these are both accessible and identifiable. Each illustrated pressure point lists its corresponding meridian followed by a list of symptoms, including emotional issues, that acupressure is reputed to address. According to the ancient Chinese maps, the body has fourteen meridians, or streams, that connect the acupressure points with a related internal organ. Which pressure point you massage during your prayer time is determined by what you want to accomplish. Choose the pressure point based on your physical or emotional needs.

Pericardium: circulation, angina, irritability

Large Intestine: abdominal pain, sore throat, nasal discharge and bleeding, bowel problems, guilt

Pericardium: circulation, angina, irritability, jealousy, regret

Triple Warmer (Glandular): thyroid, adrenal, edema, sore throat, abdominal distension

Heart: Cardiological issues, dryness of the throat, jaundice, anger, bitterness, resentment

Triple Warmer (Glandular): earache, tennis elbow, vertigo, depression, loneliness, despair

Lung: respiratory, sore throat, cold, cough, disdain, intolerance

Heart: cardiological issues, dryness of the throat, jaundice

Small Intestine: chills, back and shoulder pain, tennis elbow, sadness, mania, depression yourself. Become aware of both the massage point and the corresponding physical or emotional center that is being affected by the massage. As you do, start to focus on God. Allow your spirit to open itself to God's presence.

The first step in seeking healing from the Divine is to allow a thorough self-examination. If there are unresolved relational issues between you and God or you and others, then the symptoms are more likely to return, because the root cause has not been addressed. Continue gently massaging the pressure point, but direct your prayers toward seeking understanding. Ask God to reveal any unresolved issues and listen to your heart to see what comes up. Make a mental note of any issues that are revealed and resolve to make amends when you have finished praying.

Once you've been released from any root causes of your prayer need, it is time to devote your prayer to healing. Don't hesitate to ask God directly for divine intervention—the separation between the spirit world and ours is much thinner than we tend to believe. As you pray, listen to what God would whisper into your heart.

If you've determined in advance that you will be massaging multiple acupressure points, you may move from one point to another at any time. However, if you are seeking relief from multiple symptoms, you may want to shift from one acupressure point to another as you refocus your prayers to the next symptom.

Just one side note: Healing and cure are two different things. Many people find healing during pointed praying, but only some find themselves cured. The difference is that while healing relieves the spirit and remedies some symptoms, a cure is a physical manifestation. There is no question that the Divine steps in and brings both healings and cures, but we must always be cognizant that God is God, and we are not, and that God's ways are not our ways. Trusting that God has our best interests at heart isn't always easy, but it is always necessary.

Body Memory Prayer

I became aware of body memory when a close friend of mine, who is himself a therapist, began a course of therapy. He believed he had gone as far as he could with a particular issue using traditional therapies. His therapist recommended a woman who was trained in body memory therapy techniques, and my friend made an appointment. Later, he told me about his experience. He shared that this woman explained how traumatic memories can get trapped or localized in the muscle tissue around which the trauma took place. When these memory sites are located and massaged, the memories are often released to the conscious mind, where they can be dealt with cognitively. He shared how the body memory therapist had found where he had stored some old memories within his abdominal muscles. When she began to massage these muscles, he said he involuntarily began to cry while difficult childhood memories flooded his mind. Once he became aware of the memories and the associated emotional distress they carried, he processed them in conversation with the therapist and found that some of his old issues were put to rest.

According to body therapists, the memories we carry within our muscle tissue can create stress and tension in our lives. The secret to releasing these memories is in discovering the tensions within our bodies, massaging these sites, and then confronting whatever memories emerge.

It must be noted that body memory therapy has many more components than we are going to explore in this chapter, and body memory therapists would recommend professional treatment for serious issues. While body memory prayer is a technique we can use to deepen prayer life and come to a greater understanding of ourselves, be alert to the powerful emotions it may release. The potential for healing is great, but it must be reiterated that memories of abuse or other trauma are best dealt with under professional treatment. If you wonder during a time of body prayer whether you should continue, listen to your mind and body and the Spirit's warnings, stop, and consider seeking help. To continue on your own could traumatize you again.

FINDING BODY MEMORIES

There are a couple of ways to discover hidden body memories. The first method begins with cognizant memory: remembering what you don't remember. Although that sounds like a paradox, the explanation is simple. Remembering what you don't remember is recalling those events or times in your life when you lost your memory, specifically those traumatic moments in your life from which your body is protecting you. Many people who have been in serious accidents discover that they cannot remember the events just prior to or during the accident itself. Although we know the memory is in there somewhere—we're told that our memory catches every single event—we have no way of retrieving it. I'm not suggesting that it's necessarily helpful to try to discover these kinds of memories, but these, or other kinds of traumatic memories, could be the cause of some or much of our muscular tension, thus hindering our ability to relax and sometimes even getting in the way of healthy sleep. Indeed, these memories may hinder our spiritual lives by building up defenses or walls that keep others at a safe distance.

According to body memory therapists, these memories are typically kept in the muscle group most affected by the trauma. A good friend of mine had a motorcycle accident that mangled his ankle. I spent a good bit of time with him in the hospital and we talked about the event. He remembers riding next to a semi and realizing it was turning into his lane and that he had no place to go. The next thing he remembers is the paramedics' putting him on a stretcher and getting ready to put him into the ambulance. Although my friend probably isn't interested in recovering that lost memory, body memory theory would suggest that he could find it hiding within the muscles of his lower leg. If, however, he discovered he was being haunted by a fear of trucks or was having nightmares about the incident, spending some time in prayer while having his calf massaged would possibly reveal the memory and allow him to move past it, according to body memory therapists.

The second way of discovering body memories is to be self-aware enough to find the muscles in your body that are tense for no good reason. These are *not* the muscles that are tense because you slept wrong or because you worked out too hard. These are the muscles that have tenseness in them day after day, and you don't know why. The tissues holding memories are most likely the muscle group.

Note that some of your body memories may be located in muscle groups that you do not have quick and easy access to. For instance, it's really hard to massage your back effectively on your own. In these cases, you may want to enlist a partner to help. However, know that the effectiveness of your prayer time will be affected by the addition of a partner—for good or for ill. If you will be using a partner, this person needs to be fully informed of your intentions and should be supportive of your prayer needs.

A quick word of warning—some body therapists have been accused of helping to generate false lost memories, generally concerning childhood sexual abuse issues. These accusations have brought a measure of discredit to body memory therapy. The purpose of body memory prayer, however, is not to uncover a sordid past, but to surrender to God the obvious symptoms and causes of emotional pain that may be associated with latent memories. Uncovering body memories can be the road to forgiveness. Again, though, the recall of such memories can trigger reinjury, so be extremely cautious.

Practicing Body Memory Prayer

Body memory prayer begins with the self-discovery process. If you have memories that you know have been repressed, you likely have an idea about which muscle groups have been affected and you can begin immediately. On the other hand, if you are unsure whether or not you have memories locked into your muscles, you will want to begin exploring the tensions in your muscle groups. This is best done over a lengthy period of time, often as much as a month or more. However, when you have discovered muscle tension that seems to have no other explanation, you may begin body memory prayer.

God already knows what you're about, but it is always good to begin by being forthright. Start your prayer by centering your spirit and then enlisting support from the Divine. Close your eyes and listen to your breathing. You will want to be as fully relaxed and self-aware as possible, with your mind alert. Once you feel focused, turn your mind's eye to the Divine's presence. Share what you are trying to accomplish and solicit the Spirit's aid. As you do, begin massaging the muscle or muscle group that you suspect contains the repressed memory. If there is tenderness in the muscle, a gentle massage is called for, but if the only issue is muscle tension, then a vigorous, deep tissue massage may be helpful. The goal isn't to create pain, but to release the tension, so don't get carried away.

As you are massaging the muscle, listen to your spirit and become aware of whatever it is that flows through your mind. As it says in 2 Corinthians 10:5, "take every thought captive." Use this suggestion to prayerfully examine every thought that bubbles up from your unconscious mind. As each thought emerges, consider its validity in light of your prayer. Determine whether it is a latent memory, or just a random thought—there are plenty of *those* swimming around in our psyches. If it's not a fruitful recollection, release it from your mind and continue massaging and listening.

If, on the other hand, a memory floats into your consciousness that needs your attention, capture it in your mind. Examine the memory both prayerfully and carefully to see if it's a valid memory. There are times when an unpleasant memory surfaces and we may subconsciously add fictitious variables such as events or emotions into the memory. For instance, if you have negative feelings about your big brother who used to torture you by calling you "squirt" in front of your friends, your Freudian "id" might create a traumatic memory with him in it. For instance, your subconscious could create a memory of your brother abandoning you in an eerie forest when you were five, even though it may not have been possible for that event to have ever taken place. So handle any resurfaced memory carefully.

If you decide the recovered memory is real, lift up that memory before God. Consider what you're to do with that memory. In most cases, the next step is understanding and forgiveness. For instance, in my friend's case, the truck driver didn't see him when he changed lanes and so knocked him off his motorcycle. And although the insurance companies assigned the responsibility of the accident to the truck driver, if the latent memory was causing my friend to lose sleep, he would need to figure out what it would take to come to terms with the accident and to forgive the driver.

Only by unconditional forgiveness can a memory be fully resolved. Recovering a memory isn't about retribution or revenge—it's about healing from within, and that only happens by release.

If forgiveness is a difficult thing for you, then it's clear that you will need to spend more time in prayer. Continue the massage of the muscle group, but focus on listening to the Divine speak into your life. The time to end the prayer is when the tension is gone—physically, emotionally, and spiritually.

In those cases when forgiveness isn't forthcoming, you may need to make an appointment with a trained therapist to walk you through the process. When you come to grips with the lost, latent memories, you will discover that relaxing and sleeping come much easier.

Conclusion

Sensational prayer is unquestionably the most unorthodox of the prayer types offered in this book. As you become familiar with the various prayer types, and have practiced each of them a couple of times, you will doubtless find these prayers can help you spend inordinate amounts of time in the presence of God. And although not all of these prayer types may be your favorites, each has its place in the kinesthetic toolbox.

CHAPTER 7

Prayer Walking

I was introduced to prayer walking by the writings of Thich Nhat Hanh, a Buddhist monk, in his book *Peace Is Every Step: The Path of Mindfulness in Everyday Life* (Bantam, 1991) over a decade ago. Nhat Hanh teaches that the art of true living is found in being mindful of the present moment. His book suggested going for walks when you have no place to go, when you're not in a hurry, and taking your time to appreciate the leaves of the trees, the petals on flowers, the touch of the breeze, and the stones on the road.

The first time I set out on a "mindful walk," I was so touched with the experience that I found myself breaking into spontaneous prayer with each step. I encountered within me an incredible sense of gratitude for life and for the beauty of the world around me. By the time I had finished, my spirit was refreshed and my heart was glad.

Little did I realize that those first mindful walking steps were the beginning of an exciting spiritual journey.

The First Prayer Walks

Prayer walking has a long history that likely goes back to the earliest days of organized religion. In the ancient Mesopotamian religions, there were festivals celebrating the visitation of the gods to local towns and villages. During these celebrations the devotees would join in a procession with the god through the town—they would literally walk with their god.

The Bible uses the phrase less literally. The first person mentioned who walked with God was Enoch in Genesis 5:22–24. Generally, the phrase "walking with God" means that someone was a conscientious observer of the faith—he or she believed and then walked the talk. The story of Enoch ends not at his death, but when he was taken alive into heaven because of his righteousness. Others who walked with God include Noah and Abraham.

However, even in the Bible, walking with God implied an intimate, one-on-one relationship with the Divine. This was built on prayer and a growing, personal dialogue with God. Indeed, God called Abraham his "friend" (Isa. 41:8). Relationships like these grow when we spend time in the presence of the Divine.

Prayer Walking

There's more to prayer walking than just going for a walk—though not much. For those of us who can't sit still, going out for a prayer walk can be a welcome break in the day that not only invigorates our prayer lives, but also offers heart-healthy exercise, and can help ready our minds for whatever appointment or task is coming up next. The benefits of prayer walking are obvious, but there really is more to it than you might first imagine. There are three regularly practiced focuses of prayer walks: *devotional, intercessory,* and *spiritual warfare* walking. Devotional walking is dedicated to becoming mindful within God's presence. Intercessory walking is dedicated to praying whatever it is God sets before you. And spiritual warfare walking is dedicated to praying an agenda associated with the locale of your walk.

Devotional Prayer Walking

Of the three, devotional prayer walking is the most like Thich Nhat Hanh's description of mindful walking. The point of devotional prayer walking is just to be in God's presence and to meditate on your relationship with the Divine. It begins with no other agenda, although you might choose to bring up particular prayer needs as you walk.

To begin a devotional prayer walk, you will want to decide where you're going to walk. I'm a tree person; that is, I love to walk where there are trees, and frankly, the farther away I am from anything that looks like civilization, the happier I'll be. On the other hand, my wife is a beach person. She loves to stroll along the ocean's sandy beaches, where she can feel the wind in her hair and the sounds of the surf literally rolling over her. For the best prayer walks, frequent those places where you find yourself becoming centered intuitively. These are the places God can best speak to your spirit.

For devotional prayer walking, you will probably not want to go to places where you will be with a lot of people. Many of us are aware that the proximity of others can be a serious distraction. Even walking in your neighborhood during certain times of the day when the houses eject their charges into the front yards and streets is probably counterproductive, since the temptation may be not only to greet, but to chat with your neighbors. Remember, a devotional prayer walk is meant to be just you and God. If you are going to pray where you will be meeting a number of people, you may want to consider taking an intercessory or spiritual warfare walk instead, especially if you are one who finds yourself easily distracted.

Once you've decided where you're going to take your prayer walk, dress appropriately. There isn't much worse than going out to spend time with God, finding yourself basking in the Spirit's presence, and then realizing you're freezing and can't bask as long as you'd like. I'm not a member of the fashion police, but it seems to me that dressing in layers still has a place in our society. If it is chilly outside, or if you're walking in the late afternoon when it may turn cooler as the time progresses, take a sweater or jacket and toss it over your shoulders or tie it around your waist. Better to have it and not need it than the other way around. And don't forget to wear comfortable shoes. This isn't the time to break in the patent leather wing-tips.

Before you leave the house, you may want to consider packing a few other items in a fanny pack or a jacket pocket. Some like to carry a pocket Bible or a copy of their favorite poetry book to peruse as the spirit moves. Taking a bottle of water is also a good idea, as is a can of pepper spray if you're likely to meet an overly protective dog. If you have a cell phone, taking it along is a good safety precaution, but you may want to turn off the ringer and vibrator so that you won't be disturbed. And don't forget a walking stick or an umbrella as the terrain and climate dictates.

When you're ready to begin your prayer walk, take a moment to get centered. Centering while outdoors has always seemed easier to me than while I'm sitting in the living room. The sounds of the breeze, birds, and insects fill my ears and offer me peace. The scents of leaves, grass, pine, and fir take me to pleasant places in my mind. Take a few minutes to breathe deeply and shed yourself of nagging concerns and niggling thoughts. Feel the presence of creation around you as you take each breath. When you feel at one with yourself, begin your prayer walk.

When you do a prayer walk, you're not practicing for the Olympic speed walking team. The goal of your prayer walk transcends even aerobics—worrying about getting your heart rate up is counterproductive. Instead, walk slowly and mindfully. Be aware of your surroundings and how creation is making an impact on you.

Look.

Listen.

Smell.

Feel.

As you walk and become aware of your surroundings, turn your thoughts toward the Divine. One good way of doing this is to repeat a spiritual phrase such as a short Bible verse, a written prayer, a line or verse from a spiritual poem, or a few words from a particular song that moves you spiritually. In the book *The Way of the Pilgrim,* the anonymous author repeatedly prays the *Jesus Prayer*—"Lord Jesus Christ, Son of God, have mercy on me, a sinner"—as he makes a pilgrimage across Russia and Siberia. Other common phrases include: Psalm 46:10, "Be still, and know that I am God"; Psalm 23:1, "The LORD is my shepherd, I shall not want"; Saint Francis's prayer, "Lord, make me an instrument of thy peace"; and Saint Patrick's prayer, "Christ be with me, Christ before me, Christ behind me, Christ within me, Christ beneath me, Christ above me, Christ at my right, Christ at my left."

Another way to focus on God is to read a Bible verse or another spiritual writing and meditate on it as you walk. A verse from the Psalms or a paragraph from the spiritual writer of your choice can help you to set your inner sight on the Divine. You may choose to read and reread as you walk, or focus on a particular word, thought, or feeling that was evoked while you read. Listen to your spirit as you walk and as you meditate. Allow the sights, sounds, scents, and sensations of creation to wash over and through you as you take each step. Once again, it's about taking time with God, not rushing through your walk as if the focus was on winning a race or getting somewhere. The only "somewhere" you are trying to get is into God's presence.

As you walk, you may find yourself flooded with emotions. If you are overwhelmed with a sense of gratitude for the beauty around you, focus on that feeling and on a prayer that reflects this. If you find yourself burdened with sadness or remorse—a common emotional response on prayer walks—live with the emotions and, as you do, listen to the Spirit speak into your heart. Direction and hope is often revealed during these times when, instead of trying to avoid our true feelings, we embrace them and allow the Divine to use them to teach us wisdom, grace, and even perseverance.

Perhaps the greatest key to devotional prayer walking is to have an attitude of awareness and listening. These walks, above all else, are times in which we can "loaf" with God, times when we put away our agendas and just take time to be. We are so often caught up as human "doers" that we forget we were created as human "beings." One of our chief needs in life is to be, that is, to be mindfully aware of our own presence within our surroundings in the present moment. These times come along so seldom in the midst of our hurried lives that they are especially fruitful when we take them seriously. By taking devotional prayer walks regularly, you not only exercise your heart; you also free your soul.

Intercessory Prayer Walking

Although there are several differences between devotional and intercessory prayer walking, the primary difference can be found in the way we listen as we walk. While walking devotionally, your thoughts are on your relationship with the Divine. However, when you walk for intercession, you are walking with a specific purpose: to listen to what God reveals to you about those you pass and then to pray for them. Intercessory prayer walking is "walking on-site with insight."

Intercessory prayer means praying on someone's behalf. If, for example, you have ever lifted up a prayer for your Aunt Sue who's having surgery, then you've practiced intercessory prayer. We offer intercessory prayer whenever we pray for world peace, or for the homeless to be housed. However, when we are practicing intercessory prayer walking, we are intentionally listening for whatever God would show us, and then praying specifically about that.

Another key difference between devotional and intercessory prayer walking is where you're going to walk. Intercessory prayer walking necessitates walking where there are others to pray for. Most intercessory prayer walks are taken in the walker's own neighborhood. This is certainly one of the best places to begin, since your own personal circle of influence begins in your own home and spirals out from there to your neighbors and your neighborhood. Besides, there are few who would wish ill on their own neighborhood, so it would seem beneficial to ask for God's blessings and intervention there. However, you may also choose to do a prayer walk in a local business district or shopping area. Where you walk is up to you—so long as you'll be in the presence of others.

In undertaking an intercessory prayer walk, as you would for a devotional walk, wear appropriate clothing, take water, consider taking a Bible or prayer book, and so on. As you leave your home, center yourself. However, this time begin centering by focusing on the Divine. Since God is already working in the lives of those in your neighborhood, ask God to show you where the Spirit is working so that your prayers might be a part of God's work. Then ask God to speak as you walk and to direct your prayers.

Set out on your prayer walk by listening to your spirit. Walk slowly with your eyes and ears open for clues to how God might direct your prayers. You will want to be especially mindful of your surroundings as you take each step. Rather than listening to the sounds of nature, listen to the sounds of your neighbors and your neighborhood. Greet those you meet. Smile and be open to conversation with your neighbors, because God will often reveal where the Spirit is working in these conversations.

For instance, during one prayer walk, a friend of mine greeted a neighbor up the street, whom he had never met before. She initiated a short chat and during the conversation she somehow deduced that he was a Christian. Perhaps he was wearing a cross, carrying his pocket Bible, or maybe she'd asked him what he was doing and he told her about the prayer walk. However it was that she discovered the fact, she broke into tears and told him that she had that very morning prayed that God would send her a Christian to talk with her. My friend was literally the answer to her prayers. If he hadn't been fully present to those around him in his prayer walk, he might have missed this important need in his neighborhood.

When you're prayer walking as an intercessor, pray for each house, business, and person you pass. Look for important clues as to what to pray for. If the yard is filled with children's toys, pray both for the children and the parents. If there's a basketball hoop and a skateboard in the driveway, pray for the teenagers. As you pass businesses, pray for those who are working there and for God's guidance for the owners and management. Pray for protection of the police and the fire department as you pass, or as they pass you. If an ambulance goes by, pray for the patient and pray for the emergency workers. Simply be mindful as you go, and pray for those you pass.

The more you practice intercessory prayer walking, the more attuned you will become to the Spirit speaking to you. Listening to God is a skill that comes with practice so don't hesitate to practice it often by venturing out on these prayer walks regularly. As you do, your face will become familiar in the neighborhood and you will find people more open to your presence. Indeed, as you walk, don't be surprised to be asked about your slow, mindful walking. When asked, the best thing you can do is to be open and honest. Tell them you're prayer walking and you're praying for your neighbors and the neighborhood. If you've been praying specifically for this particular neighbor, you may want to share that. You *might* get an odd look, but more often than not, your neighbor will want to know more. Share as you feel led—this is not the time to be bashful or embarrassed about your faith.

Often, your neighbor will open up and share with you some prayer need that they have and ask you to pray about it. The typical response by most Christians is to agree to pray for the need. But for most of us, that's where it begins and ends. We are fallible humans, so we often forget to pray in a timely manner for those who ask. To get around this, and to seriously affect your neighborhood, pray for your neighbor right then and there. I seldom ask for permission—the person already asked me to pray—I simply close my eyes and begin to pray aloud. Don't worry about eloquence or about trying to sound holy. Your neighbor asked for prayer, pray using the same words the neighbor used. You might pray something like this:

> God, Fred says his teenagers are out of control and hanging around with the wrong crowd. He says he doesn't know what to do. I ask that you would send good influencers to his children; that you would help Fred to be a good, loving, and wise parent; and that he might discover peace through this difficult situation. Amen.

After you've prayed, listen to your spirit about staying and chatting or moving on to continue your prayer walk. If you are involved in a faith community, you might extend an invitation before you walk on, but unless you feel God leading otherwise, this is not the time to put pressure on anyone. You've just opened a door, and one of the best things you can do is to continue your walk and check back with your neighbor in a few days.

Some have asked how to hear God in their prayer walking. The answer isn't nearly as pat as I'm sure they would like. Hearing the Spirit's voice within seems to be unique to each one of us. Very few people I know claim to have heard God speak audibly so that they could physically hear. Most of us hear God deep within our souls. I know the Divine's voice is speaking when what I hear doesn't come from me or from the dark side of evil. Typically, what I hear isn't so much words as intuitions and leadings. For instance, as I walk, I may get an uneasy feeling in front of a particular house (for no discernible reason, such as being unhappy with the neighbor's dog). In this case, I pray for protection of the household and for a spirit of peace to intervene. Occasionally, I may sense a more specific prayer need, such as a sense that someone in the household is sick. In this case I pray for relief, for healing, and for health.

There are also times when you may feel a strong need to intercede with prayer at a particular home. If you sense a reason, then simply pray at the house and move on as the Spirit leads. However, sometimes you may feel an urge to go up and knock on the door. Of course, use common sense here. One of the best ways I've discovered to approach these times is to go to the door, knock or ring the doorbell, and then simply tell the adult who answers the door that you are one of their neighbors, that you were out walking and praying, and that you felt a leading to stop and ask if they had a need that could use some prayer. Very, very seldom will you be turned away. According to a recent poll, from the Barna Research group, eight out of ten adults claim to pray during the week, so clearly the odds are against someone thinking you're a nutcase. Most of the time, whoever answers the door will share a prayer need with you. Once again, pray then and there rather than later—it shows you take prayer seriously.

Intercessory prayer walking can literally change neighborhoods. The power of prayer is tremendous; it is probably the most underutilized tool in our faith practices. By bathing your neighborhood in prayer, you will discover your own attitudes changed toward your neighbors. Not only will they benefit from your prayers, you will find your heart moved to make a difference in your community.

Spiritual Warfare Walking

This final prayer walking technique is neither for the uninitiated nor for the timid. To engage in spiritual warfare walking is to directly confront the powers of darkness by calling on the Divine to intervene in specific circumstances. This kind of prayer walking takes preparation time as well as personal prayer time. Additionally, spiritual warfare walking is enhanced with the collaboration of others; indeed, it is best practiced with the support of others who are backing you up with their prayers. Spiritual warfare walking takes seriously the words of the apostle Paul, who wrote:

> For we wrestle not against flesh and blood, but against principalities, against powers, against the rulers of the

darkness of this world, against spiritual wickedness in high places. (Eph. 6:12, KJ21)

In other words, we have to take the battle to the spiritual realm, and one of the best ways to do that is to practice spiritual warfare walking.

Preparing for Spiritual Warfare Walking

Spiritual warfare walking begins by getting to know your neighborhood on a spiritual level. In most neighborhoods there are bastions of good and pockets of spiritual evil anywhere you care to explore. The pockets of evil can often be found in places of ill repute, places where less-than-godly activities are practiced, and places where the Divine seems to be kept at bay, for instance, drug houses and porn dealers. There are many pockets of evil in every community—your first job is to get to know your neighborhood well enough to recognize them. Sometimes these pockets of evil are so prevalent that only the spiritually blind could miss them. Certain businesses and business districts exploit and cater to the baser instincts of humanity. All these may be places where spiritual warfare walking can be effective.

Besides the obvious pockets of evil, there are less blatant clues to locales that are spiritually embattled. In your own community there are probably places where the tenor of the neighborhood is darkened because of spiritual impoverishment. These neighborhoods are not necessarily the ones that are low income; rather, they are those where evil is not only practiced, but tolerated. Some of these neighborhoods are dangerous to walk at night. Others are well lit and seem safe, but actually are harbors for immorality and impurity. The saying that you can tell a tree by its fruit is no less true here. Neighborhoods can be known by the fruits they bear. Crime, domestic abuse, divorce, alcoholism, drug addiction, and juvenile delinquency happen almost everywhere. However, there are neighborhoods where these fruits of darkness are more prevalent than in others. These communities need spiritual warfare walkers.

The practice of focused, spiritual warfare walking begins with the identification of a target for your prayer walk. This may be a particular business, business district, or neighborhood. Begin the process by "lobbing prayers" at the target from your own devotional time at home. All prayer to God is expedient, so prayers from afar are also heard and answered. Know, however, that if you are going to practice spiritual warfare walking, you are confronting the forces of darkness. Do not take this lightly. Evil is real and has real power. Although evil will not triumph in the end, in many battles being waged every day evil gets the upper hand and wreaks havoc in people's lives.

Before you actually visit the site of your spiritual warfare walk, it would be wise to recruit a spiritual friend or two or three to come along with you as prayer partners. There is indeed power in numbers, and the more focused the prayers offered, the safer the immediate environment becomes—especially to those doing the praying. Your prayer partners should be spiritually mature and fully prepared for the task at hand. This is a time for serious, heartfelt prayer offered by prayer warriors.

When you are ready to visit the site, begin by getting centered, as always. The whole group should do this before setting foot in the neighborhood. Invoking God's intervention and divine protection is a necessity that cannot be overstressed. As you will be entering the enemy's territory—like sheep among wolves (Mt. 10:16)—you will want the Good Shepherd to walk with you every step of the way.

As you arrive at the site, know that your purpose is not to disrupt the lives of the residents or the businesses. You are there to pray, nothing less and nothing more. Picketing, either with signs or by being an obnoxious presence, does not accomplish your purpose. The reality is that the more prayer you offer, the more spiritual forces you bring to bear. If you're asked to leave because you've been a nuisance, then you've hindered, not helped the cause.

Pray with your eyes open and your heart focused. Ask God to intervene with power, strength, love, and grace. Take the time to pray for the individuals who are present there. If the target is a particular business, it may be appropriate to pray for its removal. Even more effective, however, is to pray for the customers who frequent the business. Pray for their well-being, that they might receive wisdom, and that their lives would be complete. People who have these characteristics tend to avoid places of ill repute.

The focus of your prayers should be on the Divine and on God's intervention. There may be a temptation to address the powers of evil directly, but unless you are well experienced in this, resist the temptation. The real power in spiritual warfare is in prayer. Keep yourself focused on praying for God's will and God's intervention—it's the best thing you can do.

I'll close with a story that illustrates effective prayer walking. It is a good example of how to do an effective spiritual warfare walk. A friend of mine in California became concerned when a casino opened up the street from him. Over time he noticed that the temperament of the community began to erode, and so he felt the need to intentionally prayer walk the casino. He recruited a couple of friends who were spiritually mature and together they visited the establishment.

When they arrived, they looked like any other customer who might visit the place. They didn't wear clergy collars or crucifixes, they didn't carry Bibles in their hands, and they didn't have any signs. They also didn't try to dissuade the customers from going in. Instead, they went into the casino and took up separate "posts" inside. They stood out of the way, inconspicuously against the walls. Together they prayed silently, eyes open, for the customers, for the employees, and for God to intervene. Then, after an hour or so, they left.

This prayer team returned regularly to take up their posts and pray. On one occasion the manager, who knew my friend, saw him come in. He rushed over and asked him what he was doing there—the manager knew he wasn't there to patronize the gaming tables. My friend was honest and simply said he was there to pray for the customers and the employees. The manager was visibly shaken, but didn't ask them to leave.

The result of their faithful prayer walking was slow in coming. It took some months, but in the end the casino closed. The prayer team hadn't been obtrusive, nor had they been a nuisance. Instead, they had simply called on the power of prayer to tip the forces of good over darkness.

If you choose to engage in spiritual warfare walking, know what you're getting into. Spiritual warfare is messy and it can invade your own fortress. If your prayer life is strong, if your faith is stronger, and you feel the Spirit urging you to go to war, then spiritual warfare walking is an important and effective weapon in changing the face of your community.

Conclusion

Walking under the open sky in prayer is an ancient practice ("and Isaac went out to meditate in the field," Gen. 24:63, KJ21) that makes sense today. Not only will it do your heart good, not only will it do your spirit good, but it will do your community good. Keep your eyes, your ears, and your spirit attuned to the Divine as you travel, for there is much out there that needs spiritual attention, but there will be little change in our world if those who believe in prayer refuse to leave their armchairs and engage the world in prayer. So if you need a good reason to get out there and exercise, prayer walking can be your best excuse—and it can lead to some of the best results.

CHAPTER 8

Artistic Prayer

God is the ultimate artist. Look around and see the world as the Divine sees it. The watercolors of a rainbow, the sculpted majesty of mountain crags, the carving out of canyons and valleys, and the repetitive, nested fractal drawings in a single palm frond. We often picture God creating the world and then retiring, but this clearly isn't an accurate account. Each day, somewhere, millions of tiny ice crystals called snowflakes are falling from the sky—each one created with a different pattern. Each hour newborn babes enter the world—each with a different skin tone, personality, fingerprint, footprint, and so on. And astronomers have discovered that the universe appears to be expanding from some central point, where creation of the cosmos continues in an unending spewing of matter hurled into the emptiness of space to be molded into stars, planets, comets, meteors, and galaxies. God is not yet finished with the art of creation.

The Bible teaches us that all humanity, both male and female, was created in God's image. One of those images is the human as "apprentice artist." We each have a God-given creative nature within us that demands expression. Some of us are driven to paint, some to sculpt. Others express their creativity in written or spoken words. Still others do so through drama. Mathematics, engineering, invention, music, architecture, photography, programming—all are expressions of the creative nature within us.

Art is an especially necessary activity for those of us who can't sit still. We need a kinesthetic outlet for the creativity that is pent up within us. Most of us have had our creative natures caged, packaged, and confined from very early on. Gordon MacKenzie, in his book *Orbiting the Giant Hairball,* noted that when he asked a first-grade class if there were any artists there, the kids all leapt up, raised their hands, and identified themselves as artists. When he asked a second-grade class, about half would raise their hands admitting they were artists. In third grade only ten out of thirty would raise their hands—and then only tentatively. By the sixth grade maybe one or two would guardedly raise their hands. His conclusion is that the loss of our creative energy is a result of society's efforts to train us away from our foolish ways so that we can become "normal." But since those of us who can't sit still are in no way "normal" anyway, for us art can be a natural expressive outlet that should not be denied.

Art has long been used in prayer. The Greek Orthodox Church has used icons as windows to the Divine for centuries. These pictures of the Divine and the saints were gazed on as the worshipers entered into prayer. The thought was that as people meditated on the icon, they would be guided into a spiritual space where they could commune with the Divine. The same theory applies to religious frescos, stained-glass windows, sculptures, ornate altars, and the painted ceilings of the Sistine Chapel. These works of art were all used as aids to facilitate worship and prayer.

But there's more to art and prayer than just gazing upon it, especially for those who haven't had the creativity beat out of us. One of the most satisfying prayer habits is artistic prayer—prayer as expressed creativity.

Although there are many different expressions of art as creativity, this chapter will offer two of the most common types: drawing and painting. If you've had your creativity squelched by well-meaning parents, teachers, and peers, never fear. Artistic prayer is an expression of your inner heart. Your art isn't meant to be compared to anyone else's. It is uniquely yours, and whatever you create, know that it is an offering to God and is acceptable, lovely, and meaningful.

Drawing as Prayer

I'm a doodler—always have been. My artwork as such isn't much to show off, but I have a really good time producing it. In fact, when I was in college, I took a course called *Drawing for Everyone*. On the first day of class, the instructor asked each of us why we were taking the course. When I confessed that I wanted to improve my doodling, most of the class giggled. But the instructor, bless her heart, commended me and assured me that no matter what level of doodler I was, I'd finish the course much improved. She was right. I can now actually pull off perspective in my doodling!

Drawing, however, held much more potential than simply keeping my hands busy while listening to a lecture or a sermon. By taking my doodling and offering it to God as a way of praying, I discovered meaning and sometimes even purpose in my creations. Often my prayer drawings express what I can't quite put into words. For instance, in the prayer doodle on the next page, my devotional reading was Micah 7, and I was caught up in the trampling down of my sins coupled with the compassion God has for me. My soul cry was "O that it would be so" that day as I thought through the sins I had been guilty of over the previous days. The hand from heaven brings relief, though, and I wait on my island of loneliness for God to rescue me with Divine compassionate gifts.

The tools for prayer drawing are minimal: paper and pen or pencil. If you have a penchant for shading, charcoal pencils are your ticket. If it's color you crave, a box of colored pencils,

MICAH 7:19

You will Again have compassion on us
you will tread our sins underfoot
And hurl all our iniquities into the depths of the sea

O that it would be so...

PRIDE
ANGER sloth
Gluttony Lust
Envy Greed

diligence Patience
Abstinence Liberality
humility chastity
kindness

Author's prayer and drawing based on Micah 7

crayons, or felt-tipped pens can spark your imagination. A host of other drawing supplies can be picked up as well, if the creative bug bites you. Pastels, chalk, calligraphy pens, charcoal sticks, watercolor pencils, and craypas are all great for drawing; and don't forget that a wide variety of paper choices exist as well. As for me, though, I tend to doodle on whatever paper I happen to have near me. Yellow pads are my personal favorite—not because they're especially art-worthy, but because they're what I use most to take notes on. Availability is the mother of creativity.

Prayer Drawing

I doodle almost compulsively, but I take prayer more seriously than I do my doodling. So most of the time when I'm going to draw my prayers, I do so with intentionality. I recommend that you find a quiet, well-lit spot that is inspirational to you. I have a small study that doubles as a guest room that I regularly retire to when I'm going to pray. There's comfortable seating, throw pillows galore that I can use to kneel on if I'm so inclined, and a tabletop fountain my youngest daughter gave me, which helps set a prayerful tone. You will want to have a flat surface to draw on. I use a clipboard or a large book fairly regularly, but I also have a small table I can use. Having a number of inspirational writings, pictures, and symbols can also empower your creative nature. Gather your art tools around you and you're ready to begin.

There are at least three different ways to engage in drawing your prayers. Each one serves a different purpose, so your creativity never really gets stale even if you practice prayer drawing frequently. The three forms of prayer drawing I use are: drawing thoughts or prayers, meditative drawing, and spontaneous prayer drawing.

Drawing Thoughts and Prayers

This first form of drawing thoughts and prayers is one of the most frequently used. Begin by getting centered through deep breathing and relaxing. Then turn your thoughts to God before you pick up your pencil. This is a good time to do some visualizations. In your mind's eye, picture yourself in the Divine's presence. Sometimes I see myself in among the stars. At other times I visualize myself standing before a huge throne with a dazzling light emanating from it. Once you feel yourself in God's presence, try to become aware of what you're feeling. Consider what you want to bring before God. Live for a moment with these feelings and then begin to draw what you are thinking or praying.

Although different personalities demand different strokes, I would encourage you to not get hung up with trying to perfect your drawing. Instead, let the drawing express your thoughts, feelings, or prayers rather than trying to create a representation of reality. Don't worry about perspective or shading or even getting the shape down "right." Instead, let your pencil do the talking for you and don't worry about what it looks like. The point is to express yourself in the presence of the Divine.

As your prayers move from thought to thought, allow your drawing to expand into different dimensions. For instance, you may begin your prayer time sketching a scene that conveys feelings of disappointment; however, after several minutes of this you may find you've worked through the disappointment with God and discovered a sense of peace. As you find yourself moving from emotion to emotion, topic to topic, and prayer need to prayer need, simply continue drawing your prayer as an ongoing conversation and revelation of your heart. Again, the finished product is much less important than the process of expressing your spirit to the Divine.

As you wind down from your prayer time, spend a few moments looking at your creation. Encourage your soul to reexperience the feelings and prayers you have expressed. Consider what you have asked of God, whether it be a specific need or a general plea for Divine's presence, and see how you expressed that in your drawing. Then I would encourage you to date the drawing and keep it somewhere so that you can revisit your prayer, just as others who keep a prayer journal do.

Meditative Drawing

The second form of prayer drawing is meditative drawing. Meditative drawing is unique because it starts with the written word and expresses it through illustration. The doodle prayer earlier in this chapter is also an example of meditative drawing.

Although the tools of meditative drawing are the same as any other drawing type, here you begin by reading a devotional passage. I love the writings in the scriptures, so I do my drawing from Bible passages that catch my heart; however, any poetry or prose that points your heart toward the Divine is suitable for this exercise. Once again, find a peaceful place to work, find your center, and release your thoughts to the presence of God. Then take up your chosen book and read a passage thoughtfully and prayerfully. When a particular paragraph, verse, sentence, or line catches your attention, reread it and let the words wash through you. In your mind's eye, offer the passage to the Divine and listen to the voice within you. As you do, pick up your pencil and begin to sketch what you sense. Your drawing might be abstract or it might be representational (like the Divine's foot treading on my sin). There are no right or wrong ways to draw your meditations—no lines or boundaries you're required to color within. Instead, let your heart direct your fingers and your hand as you think on what you've read and what it means to you.

Don't hesitate to express your feelings as you meditate in your drawing. Hurt, anger, depression, joy, peace, and hope are all a part of our lives, and expressing them through your drawing can not only be a direct connection to God, it can be cathartic as well. Allow yourself to release your innermost self in expressing what you've read and the emotions the reading has unleashed.

When you feel you've finished your drawing and are bringing the meditative prayer to a close, take the time to explore your picture with your eyes. Allow your mind to walk through the drawing and visit the nuances of what you've drawn. Listen to your heart to see if God has a word to share through your art and if so, take a moment to respond. Then close your time by dating your drawing, annotating it with whatever passage has evoked the meditative drawing, and putting it in a file, sketchbook, or drawer for safekeeping. Reviewing these drawings, especially the powerful ones, can guide us into a deep prayer place at some future time.

Spontaneous Prayer Drawing

The third form of prayer drawing is one of the most amazement-provoking prayer types of all. This kind of prayer depends on your ability to find a centered place where you are aware of the presence of the Divine and then keep your mind focused on God while you let your inner spirit take pencil in hand. Although it can be a bit difficult at first to keep your conscious will from taking over to guide the art, the results when you are able to keep focus on God can be amazing. Most of the time the art will border on the abstract, but over time when you meditate on what you've drawn, you are likely to discern meaning and multiple levels of symbols and prayer thoughts in your creation.

To practice spontaneous prayer drawing you will need a place where you will not be distracted for a sufficient period of time. I've discovered I need to set aside at least thirty minutes, and sometimes as long as an hour, in order to get to a point where I feel released during my prayer time. Spontaneous prayer drawing takes a little more preparation than the other prayer drawing styles because of its unique challenges. Since the object of the exercise is for you to draw spontaneously without restraint, you will need a large enough "canvas" on which to work that you will be uninhibited by space. I use an 8 x 11" piece of paper and tape it to a table, desk, or easel so that I am unhindered in penciling my strokes. There are pads of newsprint and larger sketchbooks available if you feel the need for a still larger "canvas."

Once you're ready, take some time to focus on the Divine. Try to keep your thoughts directed on God and on being in God's presence. Practice deep breathing and listening for a few minutes before you get started. Ask God to make you aware of the spirit's presence. Then, when you feel fully centered, take up your pencil and make a mark. Let your hand work unfettered by your conscious mind in the beginning. Once you've made a mark (whether a curve, a line, or a shape) allow your hand to make the next line from your intuition. You may find your hand instinctively returning to continue with the first mark, or it may start something new.

As you draw, allow your mind to stay centered on the Divine's presence. The more you draw, the less spontaneous the image will become as marks become shapes and shapes become images. Allow your thoughts to take you wherever God directs and add to your drawing as you are led. Keep your mind on the presence of the Divine and on the drawing until you sense that you are completely finished. Then put your pencil down, let your mind step back from the picture, and look on it as if you were seeing if for the first time. What you discover may surprise you.

In one spontaneous drawing I made, I was dealing with some anger I had been living with and discovered I had drawn some stick figures suspended on a ladderlike shape in the center of the drawing—which appeared to be in the center of a torso. When I finished drawing, I realized that I was carrying the anger around inside of me and that it was getting in the way of my own peace and serenity. I knew from the drawing, the silent conversation with God, and from my meditation on the drawing that I needed to make some peace. I suspect that any art therapists reading this book will have a field day with this picture, but for me it was enough to discover through this spontaneous drawing that I needed to let go of what I'd been carrying pent-up inside me.

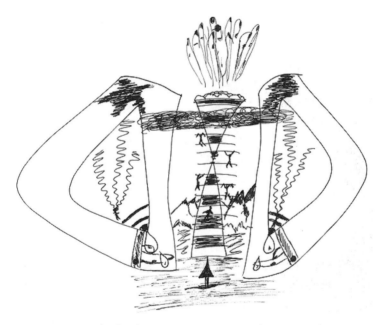

Author's spontaneous prayer drawing

Drawing prayer, regardless of which exercise you practice, has the potential to unlock the inexpressible from within you. As you can see by the illustrations I've included, the results are likely to be far from anything most might call art. But when the drawings are heartfelt and expressive, they are priceless works of prayer in the eyes of the Divine.

Painting Prayer

The difference between painting prayer and drawing prayer is primarily in the materials you'll use and the scope you can employ. Because painting often uses larger "canvases," you have the opportunity to be significantly more expansive than you generally would with a drawing prayer. Additionally, the use of paints virtually demands the addition of color into your prayer, so the magnitude of your expression is enhanced.

On the other hand, painting prayer can be significantly more time consuming and expensive than other types of prayer. Unless you are already an amateur or professional painter, there are a number of materials that you will need to secure, few of which are cheap. And yet, the results of these prayers can only be described as striking.

There are two main categories of painting prayer. The first is for the novice who hasn't studied painting and wishes only to express their prayers through the medium. The second is for those who are familiar with painting as a hobby or as a profession. Both kinds of prayer can offer fabulous expressions of your innermost prayer needs. The difference is in the presentation of the prayer.

Expressionist Painting Prayer

In the world of art, expressionism is a style of painting in which the artist attempts to express his or her feelings about some object or event. The works of art tend to lean toward abstracts, but artists like Chagall combine a number of other styles in order to express themselves. Expressionist painting is probably best suited for the novice, since the goal is to express what you're feeling rather than trying to capture what you're seeing, even if what you are seeing is only in your mind's eye.

As for the medium, watercolors are probably the best suited to the novice. Watercolors are inexpensive, particularly if you use pan (dry pigment) watercolor paints; the "canvas" is a heavy grade paper, and you can get by with only a few brushes and other supplies.

Oils and acrylics are best left to those who have either taken lessons or plan on entering the field as a long-term hobbyist. Oils can be difficult to work with and take days to dry—they're also relatively expensive. Acrylics are easier to work with and they dry much more quickly than oils, but they too can be expensive. Further, both oils and acrylics demand canvas or wood to paint on and these can be rather pricey.

If you've never before painted with watercolors, you would do well to pick up an introductory book at your public library or a bookstore. This way you can learn some of the basic techniques, such as making washes and learning to control the flow of the paints across the paper, before you begin to paint. However, for expressionistic painting prayer you can just jump in and do it—you're not going to hurt a thing.

I'm not going to deal with painting techniques—mostly because I'm not qualified. However, I do love to use watercolors in painting prayer, so here are the basics. You need paint, water, a couple of brushes, and paper. I've found the easiest watercolor paper to use is a pad of paper called a paper block. A paper block is a small stack of watercolor pages gummed together on all four sides. This keeps the paper stretched when it gets wet. (A single sheet of wet watercolor paper gets pretty wrinkled if you don't attach it to something like a block of wood until it dries.)

Basic Watercolor Tools

- Watercolor Paints (pan paints—a kid's palette is fine)
- Watercolor Brushes (#1 flat, #6 round)
- Cold-press Watercolor Paper Block (special pad of watercolor paper)
- Dinner Plate (for use as a palette)
- Cup for Water

To make a watercolor painting, take a brush full of water and brush it gently over the surface of one of the pans of paint, wetting the dry pigment into a solution you can paint with.

When your brush has enough pigment on it, brush it onto your paper. You will probably not want to use an easel to keep your paper vertical, since watercolors tend to run downhill (though there are times when you may want the paint to run!).

Use a glass or china dinner plate as a palette to mix paints on. You can create some beautiful colors from an eight-pan paint set by mixing colors on the plate. Simply take a large brush full of paint and deposit it on the plate, rinse the brush and take another large brush full of another color and deposit it next to the first color. Rinse your brush and stir portions of the paints on the plate together to create varying hues and colors.

When you're ready to paint your prayers, gather your art equipment, find an inspirational place, and set the space up for the activity. Begin by finding your centered place by closing your eyes, taking some deep breaths, and focusing your mind on the present moment. Next, turn your attention to the Divine. Get in touch with your spirit and allow your heart to be touched by God. When you feel you are in God's presence, take up your brush and begin to paint your prayers.

Because watercolors tend to bleed and run, they are the perfect medium for capturing the expression of emotions. Allow the colors and the brushstrokes to speak from your heart and soul. You can use a flat brush for broad strokes of color across the paper and a round brush to add detail. Project your prayers and your feelings onto your "canvas" by painting abstract shapes or by capturing a scene that unfolds before you. Don't worry about it looking anything like reality—even the best watercolor artists have a tough time with that. Instead, let your paints run into each other in a kaleidoscope of color.

The nature of the watercolor paints doesn't allow for perfection. Don't try to create a flawless finished product. The point of your painting is to express yourself before God, not to capture a photographic—or even an expressionistic rendering—of creation. When your heart has finished expressing itself, it is time to stop painting, regardless of the state of your "finished product." What you have produced is representative of the time of prayer spent in the presence of God. This is much more precious than any Cezanne, Constable, or Blake.

An Artist's Prayer

For those who are trained or experienced in painting, there are several ways to paint your prayers. One of the most common is to simply begin by centering yourself in the presence of God and offering every brushstroke, every daub of paint, and every moment as a gift. Paint as if you were doing so for God's sake—as if God was the patron of your art. Give in to your spirit's leading and devote the subject, the process, and the finished product to the Divine. Indeed, when you are finished, listen to your heart to see if there isn't some house of worship, charity, or person that may need your offering as a gift. Not only would this honor the Divine, but it also completes your sacrifice of prayer. The painting can essentially be a gift you offer to God.

Another way to paint your prayers is to hook up with a house of worship that will allow you to combine your artistic talent with performance art. Today, several churches have artists who produce paintings that represent the prayers of the people or the message of the pastors during the worship services. An artist will stand up front, either to the right or the left during the service, and, with back to the congregation and canvas in plain view, in about thirty minutes complete a painting that in some way illustrates the worship. By sharing their art in this way, the artists become vibrant members of the community who are connecting words to the heart through paint.

My claim to fame as an artist rests in my doodles and perhaps in my writing. My watercolor paintings lean toward the abstract, even though they are *supposed* to be paintings of barns, birds, and landscapes. But there are those, my brother included, who have talents and gifts they can use to express themselves to God in ways that make the rest of us look on in awe. In their skills and talents, their creativity, their expression, and their love of the medium, they can lose themselves in their work and present it as a sacred offering to the Divine.

Organized religion over the past few centuries has put a high premium on thought, knowledge, and science. Unfortunately, beauty, truth, and goodness were devalued, and expressing worship and communion with the Divine through the arts lost its place. Prayer became a head game that needed the right words. Artists who felt compelled to offer their creative gifts to God were left with nowhere to go and no one to affirm their heart's cry. They became divided between their religion and their art.

Today, there has been a renaissance of the arts in our society and several houses of worship have once again embraced both art and artists into their midst, giving them space, opportunity, and encouragement. This is one of the most positive signs that religion is once again finding a balance between the mind and the heart.

Other Arts as Prayer

There are many other arts that can be offered as prayer using the techniques described above. Consider sculpting prayer. This is a very popular art prayer for those of us who can't sit still, because of the kinesthetic value of molding clay in our hands. There's nothing like the feel and the scent of modeling clay as we mold our prayers into something tangible.

Creating mosaics and collages in prayer is another exciting exercise. You can get ceramic tiles or hobby glass at almost any craft store. Indeed, if you are looking for artistic prayer ideas, a walk through your local craft store will suggest literally hundreds of ways to pray using your hands and your creative nature within.

And lest we forget the most basic of basics, don't neglect the possibilities of using finger painting as an artistic prayer. For the kinesthete, this artistic expression is invaluable because you are fully connected with the paints and the paper. This is not only effective with children, but with those of any age. And besides, it's a lot of fun to make a mess of your hands!

Using art in prayer can be one of the most satisfying techniques for the kinesthete. There is something about taking inanimate objects, such as canvas or clay, and bringing them to life with our God-given creative gifts. Whether you consider yourself a professional artist, an amateur, a novice, or, like me, "all thumbs," the act of creating something as an expression of yourself before the Divine is satisfying whether you create something of aesthetic "value" or not. And frankly, if you've put your spirit into the creation, there is no art more meaningful than what you've created. Put it on display for others to see and to evoke a story of your prayer time with God.

CHAPTER 9

Musical Prayer

Historically, most of our singing prayers have been confined either to organized worship services or to songs of prayer offered in the car as we sing along with the radio. However, the opportunities for singing prayer far exceed these boundaries. I almost always have a song going through my head. Indeed, to be able to achieve the focus I needed to write this book, I either had instrumental music playing in the background or I turned on my white-noise, musical fountain that has the random sounds of harmonic wind chimes. When I leave the presence of my musical cocoon, my mind picks up a song and I find myself either humming or whistling that song no matter what I'm doing. I get a lot of smiles at the grocery store checkout lines and comments about how happy I must be—all because I carry my music, and the prayers that go with it, everywhere I go. The point is, you can do likewise.

Music isn't an add-on to the spiritual journey; rather, most of the time it is the vehicle that carries us along. Just as a movie without a sound track would consist of lifeless images pasted on celluloid, life without music would be two-dimensional and joyless. For the majority of Americans, music is simply a part of our daily lives. According to a recent study by Jim Emerson in *Direct* magazine, an estimated fifty-eight million of us play a musical instrument of some sort. As for the rest of us, we either whistle, hum, sing, or—for those who aren't confident in their ability to carry a tune—we've discovered we *can* carry a radio or a CD, audiocassette, or MP3 player. Music is part and parcel the fabric of our society. Indeed, according to a spiritual and church consultant friend of mine, music has become the ritual of our generation.

But our society didn't invent music. I suspect that if we'd been flies in the garden of Eden, we'd have heard Adam humming to himself while he pruned the roses and harvested the apricots. The first organized religions almost certainly used drums, cymbals, and horns, and when alphabets were introduced, songs and hymns were written for the world to share. Indeed, the book of Psalms in the Bible is a compendium of five hymnbooks that have been used by the Jewish faith for millennia. We don't know what the tunes were originally, but we know they were sung during worship. And the Israelites weren't the only ones with religious hymns. Hymns to various gods that predate most of the biblical writings have been recovered by archaeologists. Music and spirituality are inextricably linked throughout history.

For those of us who can't sit still, music is a particularly helpful tool for connecting with the Divine. Music is said to soothe the savage breast. When our thoughts are racing and our minds distracted, music can wash over us and lead us to a place of quiet centeredness. If we choose to play an instrument, whether we're musically gifted or not, we discover the kinesthete within us delights in our ability to shape notes or rhythms. And for those of us who love to use our voices (and who doesn't?), singing and chanting help us focus our minds on God.

Although there are hundreds of instruments, thousands of songs, and multitudes of voices, we're going to look at three main types of musical prayer-making. Singing is one of the most basic ways of praying—and you don't necessarily have to be able to carry a tune to participate. Next, for those who do have musical skills, we'll look at performing musical prayer. And finally, especially for those of us who may be musically challenged, we'll look at sound-making as prayer.

Singing Prayer

Most of the kinesthetic prayers offered in this book are useful either in worship settings or during time set aside for prayer. Singing prayer is an exception to this. You can sing almost anywhere, either aloud or silently in your mind. This makes singing your prayers one of the most effective ways to practice being in the Divine's presence all day long.

If you've ever sung a hymn at church, you've sung a prayer— even if you didn't know it. The fact is, most songs in religious settings are written prayers that have been set to music. Songs like "How Great Thou Art," and even some of the Christmas carols like "O Come, O Come Emmanuel," are written prayers. But singing prayers needn't be confined to songs contained in a church hymnbook. Almost any song, offered to God from the heart, can be a prayer. For instance, many popular love songs can be offered as prayers of our commitment to the Divine. And then there are times when a tune itself can evoke an emotional outpouring of the spirit.

Sung prayers can be taken anywhere, or everywhere, you go. You have only to turn your heart toward the Divine while you sing and remember to lift your spirit to God as you do. It is helpful to begin your singing prayers by focusing your mind on God before you begin. Take a few moments to center yourself and offer your words, thoughts, and emotions to the Spirit. Then begin. You may sing a specific spiritual song or any song that you decide reflects the prayer you want to bring to God. I tend to sing the same song over and over as I go, but when another prayer thought or song comes my way, I'll pick it up to sing for awhile. The sights I see as I travel during the day will often color or change the prayers I sing. For instance, one afternoon I was at the mall and ran into an old acquaintance. The conversation was about as superficial as it could be. Both of us were "doing great," we were both "fine, thank you," and if you'd listened to the conversation, you'd have thought we were wearing rose-colored glasses. After we parted, the pop song "Games People Play" came to my mind with its line about our never meaning what we say and never saying what we mean.

My prayer conversation revolved around the fact that not only was I not honest, but I hadn't really cared enough about the other person to inquire further and press the issue. But what if you don't know any spiritual songs? What if you don't really care to learn any? Never fear, there is an answer.

Free-Form Prayer Singing

Do you remember when you were younger and you used sit on a swing or the merry-go-round and make up songs? Sometimes we might have sung tunes we were familiar with, but most of the time they were tunes we made up that were nonrepetitive and had words that didn't rhyme. We were practicing free-form singing.

For some of us, free-form prayer singing may induce a reawakening of our innerchild—which isn't a bad thing, since we're taught that it is only through childlike faith that we enter the realm of the Divine. However, we may have to get over our artistic self-consciousness in order to practice this type of prayer. Some of us have been told that we can't carry a tune, we're tone deaf, or sound like yowling cats when we open our mouths to sing. More than one person has pointed out, however, that several psalmists wrote, "Make a joyful *noise* unto the Lord," not "sing in operatic perfect-pitch." The Divine recognizes and loves the sound of your voice—especially when you're calling out to God. When it comes to singing your prayers, God is an appreciative audience of one.

If you are self-conscious, the first few times you practice free-form singing you will probably want to be alone. And although you can practice this form of praying in your car or in the shower, I encourage you to first exercise this prayer when you can give it your undivided attention. Begin, as should be the custom for all praying, by centering yourself. Close your eyes to shut out the world around and breathe deeply—not only because this is effective for finding your center, but because your singing voice needs full breaths from your diaphragm. As you find your center, ponder over what you want to take to God in prayer. This isn't a time to make a list so much as it is an opportunity to put yourself into an appropriate frame of mind for the prayer you're going to offer. You might want to contemplate your emotional state—are you joyful or blue? Is your heart at peace, or are there underlying layers of anger? What is it that you're feeling right now? Then ask yourself why. What is the root cause of your feelings? If something's not going right, you have a direction for your prayer. If you've just experienced a blessed event that brought you joy, you have a reason for prayer.

Once you're centered and have in mind what you're bringing to God, open your eyes and open your mouth. Begin to pray aloud just like you would for any other prayer, but this time put melody and rhythm to it. As you sing, you will discover that you naturally match the tone and rhythm of your singing to your mood, and this is how it should be. Your heart naturally matches your emotions to your sung prayer, since you are singing from your spirit and not from your conscious mind.

At first your singing may sound timid. However, if you're practicing this exercise in private there is no need for bashfulness. Open your voice and sing out with all the emotional strength that is called for by your words. Honesty with the Divine is always a good policy, and your affect should match your verbalizations—in other words, your song should sound like what you're trying to express. Don't worry about what you sound like; to God your singing is as beautiful as any angelic choir. Besides, it is the heartfelt expression of your prayer that gets God's attention.

Sing your prayer as long as you have words to pray. It is perfectly okay to repeat a phrase multiple times or to let your words wander from place to place. After all, it's your song. When you feel you've come to the end of your singing, simply close with an "amen."

One of the beauties of free-form singing prayer is that it can be cathartic. As you become more comfortable with this prayer type, you will find that you put more of yourself into the song. Your emotions will begin to flow naturally and you may find yourself singing the blues loudly, or screaming out in a rock 'n' roll frenzy. This is fine, since God has big shoulders and can handle anything we dish out. Besides, if God is God, then the walls we hide our emotions behind are fully transparent to the Divine's gaze anyway. We can't hide anything from God, so why bother? Let your song pray what needs to be prayed and let God bring healing to your soul.

Chant—A Different Kind of Singing

In 1994, the monks of Santo Domingo de Silos released an album, simply titled *Chant,* that took the world of popular music by surprise. Their recordings of the monastic Gregorian chants contained a musical style that dated as far back as the eighth century and has remained virtually unchanged ever since. The fact that it received airplay on even the rock 'n' roll stations indicated how much a spiritual song was needed by the popular crowd. Although few teens memorized the words and went around singing the tunes on the bus, many would buy the album to listen to while in their rooms doing homework, thinking, or simply brooding.

Chanting has been around for a long time, certainly long before Gregory and his monastic community adopted this musical form. Indeed, the Roman governor Pliny recorded in 112 C.E. that Christians were regularly getting up before dawn to chant verses in honor of Christ, and chanting as a musical form began centuries, if not millennia, before that.

If you've never heard a musical chant, there are plenty of MP3 samples online—Amazon.com offers several. Many of the Gregorian chants are in Latin, so they aren't terribly helpful if you want to know what they mean, and sometimes the tunes are difficult. However, by listening to these chants, you can get an idea of what a chant sounds like, and there are much easier methods you can use to learn. One of these methods could be called simple-chant. This chant uses two different chant melodies of four notes each that correspond to a line in a poem or psalm. For the first line of poetry, use the first four chant notes (the first measure). For the second line of poetry, use the second measure. Then repeat for the next lines. I've tried to make learning to chant by this method relatively easy whether you can read music or not. Once you've mastered the simple-chant, you can explore further and learn any of the Taizé chants from France (see www.taize.fr) or the many Gregorian chants of the monastics.

How to Chant

There are only three things you will need to simple-chant. The first is your voice. The second is a sacred poem or one of the psalms. The third is a chant tone. There are many chant tones, but the fact is, they can be difficult to find. Because of this, I have written three chant tones for this exercise. They are illustrated below for those who read music.

The first note in each of the tones is a chant note. This means you chant the first words of the line using this same pitch. The following three notes correspond to the last three syllables of the line. I've added a rubric dot beneath the first of the syllable notes to match the example below.

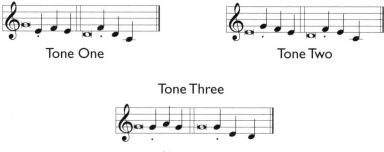

Tone One   Tone Two

Tone Three

Chant tones

The Twenty-third Psalm is one of the most famous hymns in the Bible and seemed fitting to learn as a first chant. To chant this psalm, choose one of the three chant tones and match the first four notes to the first line of the psalm, and the second measure to the second line. Then alternate the lines between the two chant tones. Remember to sing the first words (up to the last three syllables) using the chant note and the last three syllables with the syllable notes. The rubric dots are placed at the third syllable from the end of the line to make it easier to learn. Once you get the hang of it, you will be able to chant any psalm or sacred poem with relative ease. The key is remembering to sing the chant note for all the words on a line except for the last three syllables. It is only on these last three syllables of each line that you hear a tune.

> The LORD is my shepherd, I shall not be in want.
> He makes me lie down in green pastures,
> he leads me beside quiet waters,
> he restores my soul.
> He guides me in paths of righteousness for his name's
>   sake.
> Even though I walk through the valley of the shadow of
>   death,
> I will fear no evil, for you are with me;
> Your rod and your staff, they comfort me.
> You prepare a table before me in the presence of my
>   enemies.
> You anoint my head with oil; my cup overflows.
> Surely goodness and love will follow me all the days of my
>   life,
> and I will dwell in the house of the LORD forever.
>   (Ps. 23, NIV)

Praying Chants

Learning to chant may seem like a lot of work, but chanting your prayers can be a rewarding experience. To do this, begin with a prayer written in verse. Traditionally, the Psalms have been some of the most popular biblical verses for chanting prayers, but there's nothing to prevent you from choosing another sacred poem or from writing your own.

Once you've chosen a prayer, choose your chant tone to match the character of the prayer. This is a matter of personal taste, so choose whichever tone resonates within your heart. For example, I tend to use tone three for most of my personal chanting. Next, find your center by closing your eyes and listening to your breathing. You may find that humming the first chant note or the complete chant tone while you exhale may be helpful in setting the tone for your prayer time. Then open your eyes and begin to chant.

As you chant, keep attentive to the words you sing—this is the prayer that you are offering to the Divine. Remain aware of your emotional center as you chant, staying alert to feelings of sadness, joy, hope, despair, anguish, or loving devotion that may bubble up from your inner spirit. When you note these feelings, consider what is evoking these emotions. Here is where you will want to spend more time in prayer later as you work through those feelings. You may want to consider journaling after you've chanted to record and reflect on what you've experienced.

Once you've learned the techniques, chanting prayer doesn't take long to practice. I've found that chanting my prayers helps me feel a connection to the practices of the ancient saints, and points the way for me to find a place of worship in the presence of God.

Praying in Performing

I used to play in a church band with a teenager who played lead guitar. We would begin our practices with a word of prayer and then would begin working on the set for the upcoming worship service. In between songs, while the vocalists worked out harmonies and so on, the teen would close his eyes and play a few riffs that he'd been working on. The melodies he would play were seldom the screaming licks that he'd produce for most of the songs we performed. Instead, they tended to be either bluesy or gentle. When the band was ready to continue, he'd open his eyes and join in.

It was several weeks later, when he and I were chatting, that the direction of the conversation gave me the opportunity to ask him about his playing habits. He shared that when he played his guitar he was praying. He didn't pray in words and he didn't pray in images. Instead, he would express his heart through the riffs and melodies that he would pick out on the guitar.

The Christmas carol *The Little Drummer Boy* offers a similar story. A young boy without wealth comes to the manger where the baby Jesus is laying. He doesn't have gifts of gold, frankincense, or myrrh to offer. All he has his drum, so he plays as a gift to the baby. According to the song, Jesus smiled in appreciation at him and his gift. I have to believe that though the story is little more than another sentimental Christmas tradition, the moral is no less true. Our personal offerings through musical prayer please the Divine.

Since my conversation with the teenage guitar pray-er, I've practiced this prayer exercise a number of times and have been deeply moved by the experience. If you don't play an instrument, skip down to the next section—there's plenty of musical prayer that doesn't require skill in playing an instrument. But if you are one of the fifty-eight million instrumentalists, this prayer time is for you.

Begin your prayer in the company of your instrument and get it ready for playing. If you are going to use written music during your prayer, you will want to have this readily available.

Begin by getting centered and offering your playing to God. You may find that reading sacred writings is a helpful guide as you ready yourself for prayer. When you feel you are in God's presence, begin to play.

As you perform, whether you use written music, or just spontaneously compose as you go, remember that you are performing for an audience of one. This is your gift, your prayer being offered from your heart, and you will want to put your whole self into it. As you play, allow your emotions to flow to the surface through your fingers, lips, or hands. Try to focus less on the mechanics of your playing and more on expressing yourself through the music. If you are adept at your instrument and can play it literally "without thinking," you may be able to "lose yourself" in the music. Those who can lose themselves in their performance will find this place can be likened to the state of deep meditation that, typically, only contemplatives reach. Remember that the focus is on expressing yourself to the Divine through your music; therefore, try not to make perfection your goal.

It is easy to lose track of time when you practice performance prayer, so I don't recommend getting started on a day with a tight schedule. But I do recommend you give this exercise a try. There's something incredibly humbling about playing your music as a prayer for God, and it is one of the most edifying practices I know.

The Sound of Prayer

Musical prayer isn't just for musicians. As the Psalms say, "Make a joyful noise," and making noise in a pleasant pitch or rhythm is music that anyone can offer. We will look closely at a couple of instruments that I've used in prayer that are especially helpful for those of us who can't sit still, and then I finish with a litany of rhythm instruments—some of them available in your home today—that can be used effectively for this prayer exercise.

Singing Bowls

The first time I saw a singing bowl, I was at a religious conference and SERRV International (www.serrv.org) had one on display. These bowls are made of brass and come with a wooden baton. When you hold the bowl on the flat of your hand and ride the outer lip of the bowl with the baton, the bowl emits a soft note that builds in intensity as you continue to circle the perimeter. There are two kinesthetic sensations at work here. The first is the obvious movement of the hand gripping the baton and circling the bowl. The second sensation is much more subtle, but in the hands of a kinesthete extremely satisfying. As the bowl begins to "sing," it begins a light vibration that can be felt through the palm of your hand. This gentle sensation is almost mesmerizing, and coupled with the bowl's song and the circling baton,

Singing Bowl
Photo by author

those of us who can't sit still can quickly find ourselves in a very good place.

Praying with a singing bowl is a joyous experience. This is not the kind of prayer to turn to if you want to stay in a melancholy place. The lilt of the bowl will lift your spirits every time.

To pray using a singing bowl, find a comfortable place to sit and hold the bowl on the flat of your palm. Become aware of the coolness of the brass on your palm and find your center as you do. Then begin to turn your heart to the Divine as you gently run the baton around the outer edge of the bowl. As you do, the bowl will sing. The best tones are maintained by light pressure and making fairly slow revolutions—the vibrations can get erratic if you go too fast and the bowl will make less-than-pleasant sounds. As you rotate the baton and the bowl sings, allow your spirit to dance on the sounds. This exercise is a great opportunity to express joy and contentment to God, and also an excellent tool for lifting a saddened spirit. Simply let the sound of the bowl wash through you and, as it does, present whatever it is that is dampening your spirits before the Divine.

Between the two, you can count on your spirit finding a more joyous place.

Chimes

My backyard has several wind chimes that I have the pleasure of listening to on a regular basis. The sounds of the wind in the the chimes remind me that the Spirit moves wherever it will and that it can move through me when I'm open to the Divine presence. But you can use chimes as a prayer tool even without the wind. All you need is a set of harmonic wind chimes or a set of six to eight stemmed wine goblets (crystal or very thin glass makes the best sound), and some sort of baton to strike the "chimes" with.

If you're going to use goblets, take them to wherever you plan on praying and set them in place before you add water from a pitcher. Vary the level of the water in each goblet so that you get pleasing sounds when you tap the goblets with your baton. Add or remove water from each goblet until you can tap your baton from glass to glass and get a variety of enchanting musical notes from them.

If you're going to use a wind chime, you will probably want to hang it up from some sort of a stand so that you don't have to hold it up the whole time you're in prayer. If you are praying out of doors, consider hanging the chimes from a low tree branch. If you are indoors, you might hang them from a floor lamp or a plant hook. Whatever you use, you will want the chimes to be just below eye level in order to play them while you pray.

To pray using your chimes, make yourself comfortable and spend a few moments getting centered. Listen to your breathing to help yourself relax as you get ready for prayer. Then begin playing your chimes with the baton. You will not want to strike the chimes very hard, especially if you're using goblets. The object of your playing is to create a gentle, wistful sound that is reminiscent of a gentle summer's breeze. Don't try to make a song from the chimes. Instead, let your baton move randomly between the chimes, releasing melodic harmonies that sweep through you. Vary the rhythms, the tones, and the strength of your striking (*not too hard!*) to compose music that calms and soothes your spirit.

As you play, you may want to imagine the sounds of the chimes to be like the movement of God through the air. As the sounds reach your ears, let them sway and dance through your heart, taking your prayer needs and thoughts before the Divine.

Playing the chimes lends itself to calming your heart after a difficult encounter. The sounds can help you to gently release your tensions, anxieties, and worries before God. You will want to allow yourself sufficient time for playing the chimes as you pray, since in today's hectic world we seldom have enough time to release our angst. The opportunity to intentionally surrender your worries is a gift you will want to explore.

Rhythm Instrument Prayer

There are more rhythm instruments than there are pages in this book, and every one of them can be used in prayer. From drum kits to maracas, tambourines to spoons, there is a rhythm instrument out there that you can afford and use in your prayers.

The rhythm instrument that I like best for prayer is me. For the kinesthete, touch is the ultimate sensation and there's something satisfying about clapping, stomping, and slapping your legs to make rhythms. As kids, most of us discovered the wide range of sounds we can produce by gently slapping different parts of our bodies. I have a friend who taps his cheeks while holding his mouth just right to make musical sounds. I'm not so talented. But I *can* get a good rhythm going on my thighs. There are two other ways I've experienced rhythm prayer. The first is praying rhythmically and the second is rhythm performance prayer.

RHYTHMIC PRAYER

When I pray rhythmically, I tend to use written prayers, sacred poetry, and sometimes prose. I haven't had much success in creating rhythmic words and phrases spontaneously, but you may have that ability. (I am amazed at the spontaneity that young rappers seem to have when they engage their art.)

If you, like me, don't feel you can "make it up as you go," choose a poem, psalm, or other sacred writing that you want to pray. Then, as always, find your center. This is important any time you are praying, but particularly when you're going to be praying previously written material. If you can't find your center, the words you recite will lack meaning and integrity.

Once you are centered, begin pounding out a rhythm. Use whatever rhythm catches your fancy, but it should probably reflect the tenor of your prayer. If you are dealing with depression or anger, your rhythms should match your feelings. The same goes for feelings of joy or contentment. Whatever the rhythm, once you have it started, begin to read or recite the words of your prayer to the beat you are creating. As you pray, you may want to repeat a word, a line, or a verse to keep in time with the rhythm or to create emphasis. There are no rules; you're simply offering your prayers to the Divine within the framework of your rhythms.

You can offer rhythm prayers in time with almost any instrument. Indeed, it is a lot of fun to do this exercise in a drum circle or with a couple of friends who each have different instruments. When you pray this way as a community, you will want to have a leader who sets the initial rhythm, but you will discover that the rhythms change as you take up new poems or songs.

Rhythm Performance Prayer

The story of "The Little Drummer Boy" probably fits here better than anywhere else. Performing prayer for God is one of the most self-giving offerings you can undertake. To practice performance prayer, your goal is to put yourself into the music and to let the performance speak to the Divine on your behalf.

The principles of rhythm performance prayer are similar to those of the other performance prayers offered in this chapter.

Begin by centering, offer yourself and your performance as a gift to God, and then pour your heart into it. Allow your performance to express your emotions, whether they be love, compassion, gratitude, or disappointment.

Conclusion

There are almost infinite ways to offer musical prayer to the Divine. From whistling to chanting, singing to playing, the opportunities are there even for those who cannot carry a tune. The exercises in this chapter can express the full range of emotions that you may experience. Experiment with the different activities to see which ones best express your heart, whether you find yourself in the doldrums or in the clouds.

CHAPTER 10

Technology-assisted Prayer

Before I was diagnosed with ADHD, I would use the argument that I could sit for hours at a time on a given project without shifting my attention, getting bored, or walking away; therefore, I couldn't be ADHD. It didn't matter that I bounced my knee, vibrating the whole house while I was doing it—I wasn't ADHD. We've probably all known children who couldn't sit still five minutes with a math book, yet could spend five hours playing a *Super Mario Brothers* video game without looking up. And today, one of the chief complaints is that kids get into a chat room online, and would spend all their waking hours there if the parents would let them (and unfortunately, some do—it's infinitely easier than having to parent a child with ADHD). Why can some children who can't sit still for more than a few minutes doing homework find themselves glued to a movie, a video game, or the computer for hours on end? Because what they're doing (1) interests them and (2) highly stimulates their senses. Obviously, not all children who prefer video games to homework have ADHD. My point is that people with ADHD are often able to stay focused on something that interests them. Let's face it, very few of us can stay riveted to something we're not interested in. Even the most disciplined person will find his or her mind wandering when confronted with an interminable lecture or a lengthy book on the genetic differences between the male and female prairie warbler when exposed to ultraviolet B rays of exactly three-hundred nanometers for seven minutes a day (with apologies to ornithologists everywhere). That's about the same level of boredom that occurs when we tell our kids with ADHD that we're going to bow our heads and pray—and then the prayer leader switches his vocabulary to Victorian English and the content to Victorian values. The kids (myself included) stay onboard for maybe thirty seconds at best. If there's no interest, there's no attention.

But beyond boredom, it's the level of stimulation provided by technology that's important in this chapter. Of all the content in this book, praying with technological assistance has the potential to make the biggest difference in our prayer lives. When all else fails, open up the laptop.

Technology—Friend or Foe?

As part of the leadership in my religious community, I am privy to conversations about technology and the church on a regular basis. For decades I've heard complaints about technology invading our lives, and especially invading our churches. I've endured campaigns against having a television monitor in the sanctuary when someone wanted to show a clip from a video to illustrate a point. Never mind that 100 percent of those in the congregation have a VCR and a color television in their homes. I've heard screams of protest about putting a computer in the church office. It's as if technology were anti-God. I suppose the same was said when the printing press came about. And radio. And we'll be saying it about whatever comes next.

The fact is, as a society, we have always adopted and adapted technology to serve the needs of the religious communities—it just takes longer than in society at large. I've heard estimates that the church is always twenty-five years behind the cultural curve, and whatever is adopted as the norm in society today will be a part of the church in about twenty-five years. The fact is, technology is neither our friend nor our enemy. Technology is neutral. What we do with it is the matter for morality.

The internet offers a dichotomy of sites: interactive and not. For those of us who can't sit still, the interactive sites are often the most rewarding. I call prayer at these sites "Guided Prayer Tours," since these Web pages tend to be more technologically advanced and will carry you along in prayer. The less interactive sites, however, can offer incredible prayer opportunities. And though they are less glitzy, they can lead to deep and meaningful prayer times. I've described these Web pages under the heading "Self-Guided Prayer Tours." One note: although chat rooms are about as interactive as they come, they seldom, if ever, offer guided prayers, so I've placed them in the Self-Guided section.

Online Guided Prayer Tours

According to Alexa Internet, a subsidiary of Amazon.com, 1.5 million Web pages were being added to the Internet each day in 1998 (*Business Wire,* August 31, 1998). With that kind of volume, you can be sure that whatever I write for this chapter, including that statistic, will be badly outdated by the time you're reading this. However, the sites that I am choosing are sites that have either been around for a while, or are associated with entities larger than someone's family computer. The exciting thing about the wealth of Web pages being added is that with a simple search, you can discover more—and perhaps even better—Web sites than what I've offered. However, the principles of technology-assisted praying will probably not change much until technology adds something completely different (such as holograms or molecular transference).

Guided prayer tours are online sites that literally guide you through the process of praying. Some of them use Macromedia's Flash as their medium, while others use JavaScript or other scripting programs to invite you to move from "room to room" on a prayer journey. The beauty of these sites is that they tend to be visually and audibly stimulating, though they don't always demand much in the way of tactile response.

Praying a Guided Tour

To travel on a guided prayer tour, you will need a couple of tools. The first, of course, is a computer with access to the Internet. Most of these interactive sites are bandwidth heavy, so for the best results you will want to have broadband access to the Net. If you are limited to dial-up at home and you want to participate in one of these tours, you may want to visit your public library. Almost all libraries in the U.S. today have broadband access to the Internet and provide public computers for their users—all you need is a library card.

If you are going to use your office computer, you will want to check that the server will allow Macromedia's Flash. (You will also want to be careful to adhere to company rules about computer use during work time; using work hours rather than lunchtime or after work to surf the Web is one of the newest forms of employee theft.) Although most Internet browsers come with Flash installed, there are still institutions that restrict the use of second party browser plug-ins and upgrades. If your company's computers do not support Flash, you will be limited in what you are able to view.

Most of the sites that provide guided prayer tours will walk you through the process of getting centered and then into prayer itself. However, for those that don't, take a few moments for reflection and centering before you crack open your laptop or begin surfing the Web. Because the Internet is *so* stimulating, it can be difficult to find a centered place once you've launched your Internet browser.

Here are some general tips about praying guided prayer tours online:

1. Do get centered before you turn on your computer or open your Web browser.

2. Navigate directly to the guided tour Web page if possible. Avoid distractions like e-mail, banner ads, pop-ups, etc., before you've spent time in prayer.

3. Take your time as you pray. Some of these sites allow you to set the pace on the tour. You're not in a race to get done— your prayers are meant to take you into the presence of the Divine: Why hurry?

4. When you are finished, take some time to reflect on what you've just experienced. In the self-guided section there are recommended sites that encourage prayer journaling. Consider surfing there next to complete your time with God.

5. Finally, when you're done, resist the urge to immediately start surfing the Net for the next hot thing (whether that be the newest game or the hottest technology). Remember, you've been on holy ground. Steering clear of the less-than-holy, let alone the *much*-less-than-holy, is a good discipline to get into.

Online Labyrinth Walks

As I pointed out in chapter 4, labyrinth walking is an awesome kinesthetic experience. However, with the advent of online labyrinths, you don't have to leave your home or wait until a local organization builds a labyrinth in its activity room. There are two very different online labyrinths; both are interactive, but each serves different style prayer needs.

Grace Cathedral's online labyrinth is a mouse-driven miniature replica of the Chartres labyrinth in Chartres Cathedral in France. You can access this labyrinth at www.gracecathedral.org/labyrinth/interactions/index.shtml.

To pray this labyrinth, begin by choosing your icon (you can use the typical hand icon or choose a dove or gold orb) and then turning the "text" option on. The text will guide you through the labyrinth with suggestions about getting centered, releasing extraneous thoughts, and so on. To "walk" the labyrinth, take your mouse in hand and guide the icon along the path. I have a laptop with a finger touch pad that helps to simulate the exercise as if I were using a finger labyrinth. For me, this raises my tactile awareness to the journey and helps me to focus on my reflections.

The second online labyrinth is completely different from the Grace labyrinth. This labyrinth was produced by three London alternative worship groups: Grace, LOPE, and Epicentre. These groups have put together both a physical labyrinth that tours Great Britain, and an online version that is available to us all. The physical labyrinth was a temporary endeavor built on the floor of Saint Paul's Cathedral in London. Since the floor was constructed of eighteen-inch tiles, the labyrinth team used these to design the labyrinth rather than trying to impose a circular pattern onto the square tiles.

To enhance the labyrinth walk, they created eleven stations that included music, meditations, art, multimedia, and other activities throughout. Participants listened to a specially created CD through headsets as they walked to enhance the journey.

According to the creators, the online labyrinth is as close to a faithful reproduction of the full-sized one as is digitally possible. Indeed, the prayer journey is as much of a guided tour as you could possible hope for given the level of technology on the Internet. You can access the site at www.yfc.co.uk/labyrinth/online.html.

To pray this labyrinth, navigate to the site and follow the instructions. The creators go so far as to ask you to remove your shoes, as if you were going to walk the physical labyrinth in London. I have to confess that doing this heightens the sense of the holy presence as you travel. Before you enter the labyrinth, you should recognize that you are beginning a forty-minute journey if you participate fully. Although you *can* rush it, you will miss much of the mystery and the meaning. As each of the eleven stations open, there is a narration that guides you through the prayer time. Each station offers a variety of opportunities for interaction. Move your cursor around the page and explore. Some pages have surprising opportunities for interaction, while others are guided. Again, don't be in a hurry. There is much to see and do on this site and lots of prayer activities to engage in.

Online Devotional Prayer

If you don't have forty minutes to engage in an online guided prayer tour, you might want to consider the Irish Jesuits' *Sacred Space* guided meditation and prayer site. This site can be reached at www.jesuit.ie/prayer. This site isn't as interactive as the two labyrinth sites, but it does a good job of starting where you are spiritually and guiding you to a place of introspective prayer. Each step takes you a little bit deeper into the Divine's presence by peeling away the distractions from around and within you. On every page there are prayer guides to help you if you're spiritually stuck and unable to engage. These guides are different each day, so don't hesitate to revisit them on your successive visits. Additionally, there are helps at the scripture reading page in case you find yourself uninspired.

Although there are literally hundreds of devotional prayer Web sites out there, this one is probably the best I've come across. Though there is no music and no animation, the pages exude a serenity that is almost unmatched at other sites. Additionally, the prayer helps are some of the best-written inspirational invitations that I've read to date. Unless I'm really in a dark place, this site seldom fails to lift my spirit into a sacred space.

Online Worship

To many of us, the word *church* is spelled "b-o-r-i-n-g" or "i-r-r-e-l-e-v-a-n-t." This isn't the way it's supposed to be, but that's how many of us respond. But what if church—worship, prayer, sermon, and all—was online? What if the sermons were short, graphics-laden, and meaningful? What if you could celebrate communion in your own home and have the benefit of prayers and blessings? And what if you could go anytime, night or day, to worship? If participating in a guided prayer tour that includes worship sounds intriguing, then www.AlphaChurch.org is the place for you.

AlphaChurch was founded as the first fully online church in 1999 by the Reverend Patricia E. Walker in Albuquerque, New Mexico. Her goal was to start an online full-service church that could meet the spiritual needs of people across the globe. Using Macromedia Flash as her primary vehicle, she has succeeded in building a church with membership from around the world. She reports the church receives about one-and-a-half million hits each week, has about six thousand regular participants, and has over one hundred participating members, who have officially joined AlphaChurch online.

AlphaChurch has two main pages for guided prayer tours. The first is the "Worship Central" page that has the weekly service on it, as well as an archive of previous sermons (just in case you visit more than once a week). Rev. Walker's messages are complete with music and changing images that relate to the topic at hand, a veritable feast for stimulation-hungry minds. The messages are relatively short and end in a prayer time that calls for a time of reflection.

The second guided prayer tour page is called "Sacred Time." On this page you will find two communion services. You can participate in these services by bringing communion elements of bread (crackers, etc.) and wine (or juice) with you to the service. Then simply point your browser to the Web page and begin. The service is self-contained and thoughtful.

To enjoy maximum benefit of your time at AlphaChurch, I recommend beginning by lighting a candle and spending a few minutes finding your center before you begin. The lack of a quiet prayer place that leads you to the presence of God is probably the only deficit on the Web site, but if you've read this far, you are already well equipped to do this on your own. When you have finished the AlphaChurch worship service, you may want to reflect on what you've experienced by drawing prayer or journaling.

There is also a prayer page for submitting your prayer needs to the whole AlphaChurch community. If you would like to be a part of their prayer ministry, you can get connected with the newsletter, which brings bi-weekly prayer requests from around the globe to your in-box.

Guided prayer tours can be very powerful tools in your prayer life. However, there are times when you will want to spend time self-directing your own prayers. For those occasions, this next section is for you.

Online Self-Guided Prayer

Online self-guided prayer includes those sites that don't take you by the hand and lead you into God's presence. These sites do, however, offer an opportunity to enter deeply into prayer and, in some ways, can be more interactive than even the "interactive" pages above. I've chosen three online self-guided prayer sites for your perusal, but, once again, there are literally hundreds of these sites on the Web.

Online Prayer Journaling

Online prayer journaling is not for the bashful. To publicly post your prayer thoughts for all to see can be intimidating and unnerving, especially if someone else makes a comment on what you've written. On the other hand, publicly putting your faith journey out where everyone can see is also a freeing exercise. When you know the world will see your words and hear your heart, there is a sense that you are not alone in your struggles— particularly if you have read others' prayer thoughts.

Probably the best online resource for prayer journaling is to use one of the blog sites to post prayer musings (see chapter 1, *The Joy of Journaling*, for more information on blogging). The most popular site for blogging is www.blogger.com. There you can open your own blog Web page and post your prayers for all to see.

Before you begin your prayer journaling endeavor, go back and review chapter 1 on journaling. There you will be reminded of the different kinds of prayer journaling, including R^3 journaling, devotional and event journaling, and others. If you decide to engage in devotional journaling, you will want to have your sacred writings at hand to read and ponder. On the other hand, if you will be journaling a prayer to God or a conversation, then you are ready to begin.

To create an online prayer journal entry, begin by finding your center. As I suggested earlier in this chapter, especially for those of who can't sit still and who get distracted easily, this is best accomplished *before* you begin surfing the Web. Focus your heart on the Divine and then surf your way to whatever Web page you plan to use and log on. From there, let the Spirit take your mind and your fingers wherever it leads!

Bulletin Board Prayer

One of the first interactive Web services for the public was the online bulletin board. These boards popped up all over and when the churches got a hold of them, they were adapted so people could post their prayer requests and others could see them and pray about the needs. Today, there are literally thousands of bulletin board prayer sites that you can access to post your prayers online.

The best way to find a prayer bulletin board that you feel akin to is to use one of the search engines online. However, prayer sites like www.prayerboard.com and www.vurch.com have been around for a while and are easy to use. Indeed, vurch.com has an option for posting your prayer directly to God, i.e., it disappears into the electron abyss and is shared only by you and the Divine.

Once you've found a bulletin board, the next step is to compose your prayer thought. Allow your heart to make a direct connection with your fingers and let them fly. The beauty of electronic praying is that you can always go back and edit, delete, or change what you've written. When you have finished writing, take some time to read and reread what you've committed to God. Meditate for a few moments and listen to the voice in your heart to see if there is something you're being called to do about your prayer. Is there someone you need to forgive? a habit you need to change? a person you need to reach out to? If there is, this would be a good time to write a commitment as a response to the prayer. When you're done, click the "post" button to publish the request for all to see, or, if you're on vurch.com, you can click *"Just God and the Heavenly Host,"* and the post will be gone.

One of the benefits of posting your prayers on these bulletin boards is that others will see your request and have the option to pray for you. There is something to be said for multitudes taking up a prayer on your behalf. And while you're there on the site, consider taking the time to pray for others who have posted their prayer needs for the world to see.

There is one other prayer site that I want to mention. When we post our prayers online, we are using the Internet as a huge bulletin board to place a virtual sticky note on a virtual wall for others to see. We publish our requests with the hope that people from around the globe will come to the wall, read our electronically expressed needs, and join us in our prayer. Almost two thousand years ago, a real wall became the public bulletin board for prayer and it's been in use ever since. The Western Wall, sometimes called the Wailing Wall, in Jerusalem has been a sacred site for prayer since the end of the first century. This wall is all that remains intact of the Israelite temple that was destroyed by the Romans in the first century and is considered one of the most holy sites by both practicing Jews and Messianic Jews. At any time of the day or night there is a gathering of men who put written prayer requests into the spaces between the wall's stones and make the requests before the Divine. Then, once each month, the rabbis collect the requests from the wall, pray over them en masse, and burn them as an offering before God.

The Web site www.thegoldenreport.com is operated by a Messianic Jew who lives in Jerusalem. Every week Jerry visits the Western Wall and takes with him a printout of prayer requests from all over the world. These requests have come from people who have visited his site and posted their prayer needs to him. He prays over these requests and places them in the wall, where they remain until the rabbis remove them and pray over them.

You can add your prayers to this Web site just as you would any bulletin board site, except that the prayer requests are not posted for the world to view. Instead, Jerry receives it as an e-mail and will take it with him when he goes to pray. It's a different kind of technologically assisted prayer, but it seems to do a nice job of marrying the ancient with the contemporary.

Chat Room Prayer

I've saved chat room prayer for the last entry because it is the only prayer style I chose for this book that needs more than one person in order to practice it. Chat rooms have become very popular over the last several years because they offer the opportunity for conversations with multiple people from around the world in real time. Chat rooms are online gathering places where, in theory, everyone hears everyone else's conversation at the same time and anyone in the chat room can respond to everyone's conversation. It's kind of like being ADHD in a restaurant—you hear everyone around you simultaneously, but in a chat room it's not impolite to join the conversation with the folks at the next table.

There are many, many chat rooms, but many, if not most, are less than edifying unless you're looking for an Internet boy- or girlfriend. However, there are a number of public chat rooms dedicated to prayer. Some have scheduled times in which to meet a host, while others are unmoderated and depend on folks dropping by and finding each other by chance or by appointment. Still other sites have enough people visiting them that you can count on somebody being in the room when you get there.

One of the better prayer-oriented public chat rooms is found at www.churchusa.com. Their chat room is actually dedicated to prayer and there are regularly a number of visitors online. Another chat room site of note is at www.crosswalk.com. This is a well-run chat room that has scheduled prayer times during the week.

To practice chat room prayer, you will need a partner to pray with. There are a number of ways to find a partner for prayer, for instance visiting a prayer chat room when there are others present. You could also schedule a time with a friend or two in a private chat room (available at www.yahoo.com), or you could enter a chat room and simply ask if there's anyone willing to pray with you (and then retire to either an empty or private chat room). Once you have a prayer partner or several partners, allow the practice of prayer to flow naturally between you. Chat room prayer should be conversational, as if the Divine was a *lurker* (someone who is *in* a chat room, but does not participate) in the chat room—for, God is indeed in there. As others offer their prayer needs, feel free to add your "amen" or to expand on the prayer. The joy of sharing your prayers together, and both knowing and watching others praying for you, can help make your time in God's presence more meaningful than you might be able to imagine.

Conclusion

Technology continues to flourish and new technology-assisted prayer methods will continue to be created as time goes by. Who knows, maybe one day we'll be able to choose a computer-generated, holographic prayer partner like the apostle Paul or some other hero of the faith. Until then, those of us who can't sit still will continue to look for new and kinesthetic prayer techniques to bring us closer to the presence of God.

Parting Thoughts

A friend of mine who was perusing this manuscript while I was working on it asked me if my intention was to write a book that was solely helpful to those adults with ADHD. I assured her that this wasn't the case, but that the book applied to anyone who might want to experience a variety of kinesthetic prayers. However, I went on to say that as I wrote this book, my heart went out to all of my friends, both met and unmet, who can't sit still. I hope, for all of them, this book will be particularly helpful.

Many of the exercises in this book have been kid-tested. Children as young as eight years old have walked a yarn labyrinth and found God in the midst of it. We've led kids in drawing prayer and a number of the action prayers and have seen incredible connections made. I invite you to use this book as a primer for children and youth events. I've discovered that children's faith in God through prayer is often head-and-shoulders above their adult leaders, but we don't regularly offer children an opportunity to pray in a way that has meaning to them. At your next children or youth worship or activity planning meeting, consider using one of the prayer exercises to see how it goes. And then let me know. I'd love to hear about your children and youth prayer experiences.

Every time I finish a book, there's a sense that assures me there was more to write than what I got down on paper. Everyday I keep my eyes open to see if there is something I can learn about prayer that will bring me closer to God, and even during the writing of this book, new ways kept popping up.

One of my favorite books, *The Practice of the Presence of God* (Barbour & Co., 1993), is a collection of letters by a monk named Lawrence and reminiscences by his abbot. Brother Lawrence, after years of seeking the Divine's presence, discovers that the presence is always there; it's just a matter of recognizing it. This would be my own goal—to find a way to be aware of that presence all day long. That was also the goal of this book.

I hope that these writings will inspire you to take contemplative prayer seriously, even if you haven't been able to sit still for more than ten minutes in your life. Try a different exercise once a week or so and discover which ones make sense to you. If some method feels particularly *uncomfortable,* consider the possibility that there's some force at work that would want to keep you from practicing that method. Try the exercise again a couple of times before you write it off as "not your style." You might discover it is more effective than you could imagine.

After Afterword

Even as I write, more technology pushes its way to the fore and I just had to share it before I closed. One of the newest innovations you can use in your prayer journaling is audio-blogging. This new medium is available from www.blogger.com and means that you can do reflective prayer journaling while you're taking a walk (if you have a cell phone). This is one of those techniques that could enhance several other kinesthetic prayer styles. Imagine audio-journaling while sitting and praying in the center of a labyrinth. Take your cell phone with you and journal your prayer thoughts as you pass someone God has spoken to you about. Or you could audio-journal immediately after an event in your life that the Divine has used to teach or guide you. The possibilities are almost endless.

Keep your eyes and ears open to the expansion of the Internet and consider how each might be used in prayer. Then let me know what you discover—I'm always looking for new and meaningful ways to pray. If you discover new ways of praying, whether they are technological like audio-blogging, or as old as the Irish caim prayers, please let me know. You can e-mail me at pbtb@hcna.us.